THE
FUTURE
IS
SMART

THE
FUTURE
IS
SMART

THE FUTURE IS SMART

HOW YOUR COMPANY CAN CAPITALIZE
ON THE INTERNET OF THINGS—
AND WIN IN A CONNECTED ECONOMY

W. DAVID STEPHENSON

HarperCollins
Leadership

AN IMPRINT OF HarperCollins

Published by HarperCollins Leadership, an imprint of HarperCollins.

Book design by Elyse Strongin, Neuwirth & Associates.

ISBN 978-0-8144-3977-7 (eBook)

Library of Congress Cataloging-in-Publication Data

Names: Stephenson, W. David, author.

Title: The future is smart : how your company can capitalize on the Internet of things--and win in a connected economy / W. David Stephenson.
Description: New York : American Management Association, [2018] | Includes index.
Identifiers: LCCN 2018008178 (print) | LCCN 2018010249 (ebook) | ISBN 9780814439784 (ebook) | ISBN 9780814439777 (hardcover)
Subjects: LCSH: Technological innovations--Management. | Internet of things. | New products. | Strategic planning.
Classification: LCC HD45 (ebook) | LCC HD45 .S8165 2018 (print) | DDC 004.67/8068--dc23
LC record available at https://lccn.loc.gov/2018008178

ISBN 978-0-8144-3978-4 (HC)
ISBN 978-1-4002-4607-6 (SC)

To my sons:
Alex, Nat, Jared, and Jeremy

And my grandchildren:
Grace, Harper, Inti, Jack, Samantha, and Sophie

Their lives will be enriched by the Internet of Things,
provided we develop it wisely.

CONTENTS

FOREWORD

The potential growth that the Internet of Things (IoT) brings to any sector, any company, and even any citizen is undeniable. The vision of an intelligent world, with sensor-filled cities and companies, allows us to imagine a more efficient, habitable, safe, and resilient world. We are experiencing the transition caused by a merger between the physical and digital worlds, we are facing the fourth industrial revolution, and we are just starting to "lay the railroad tracks" that will make it possible.

By now, everyone in the tech industry has realized that it is not a matter of IF but WHEN it is going to explode. But as an IoT company that prides itself on frequently partnering with well-established companies, we at Libelium have learned that not all companies immediately understand the IoT's benefits— and challenges. *The Future Is Smart* will be a handy tool to help convince these skeptics how the IoT will aid them—or leave them in the dust if they don't begin to embrace it.

This is also the first time that we have experienced an industrial revolution within a digital era, making it more challenging for executives of older companies to adapt. Technology evolves quickly without a hint of a standard to adopt, and the myriad of communication protocols, sensors, and cloud platforms overwhelms even the biggest companies. And just when you think you have found all the pieces, you realize that you also need domain experts to analyze the data and that cooperation is absolutely essential. The power of the ecosystem and your ability to integrate it inside and outside your company drives the battle for the IoT's interoperability, in which some of us try to shed light by bridging hardware devices and software services.

After twelve years in this market leading Libelium as CEO—even before the IoT was a term—I have seen the multiple sides of this revolution, such as cost-savings in factories, production increases in agriculture, enhanced safety in roads, forest fire detection, monitoring and reducing pollution, and increased quality of life for citizens. In short, technology is a tool that benefits economic growth, creates jobs—yes, no doubt here—increases demand, improves production processes, and stimulates the new generation of business models.

But this promise also brings challenges, which *The Future Is Smart* emphasizes.

The perversion of technology's use and its applications, especially as they affect personal and corporate privacy and security, is evolving faster than we are able to adapt to. The Cambridge Analytica scandal exposed the boundaries between giving up on privacy and manipulation. It involves trade-offs. Last year, a drone manufacturer defined no-fly zones in some countries to prevent them from being used in terrorist attacks, which also restricted the potential use of these devices for sending humanitarian aid. Before going further on autonomous vehicles, we should first decide whose lives, motorist or pedestrian, we want to protect first. We should not allow technology to advance faster than our ethical decisions, and we need tons of awareness for that. Stephenson's decision to make privacy and security the first of his IoT "Essential Truths" drives that home.

Access to more data forces us and our companies to be more rational by installing what I expect to be the *datocracy* era. Because it is no longer *only* about gathering data but about giving a context to transform it into useful and valid information. The major challenge is not just to lead the change in our organizations to take advantage—or sometimes just to survive—in this new world but also how we decide to use and share daily technology. This new era can promote transparency in government decisions and thus, hopefully, the biggest legacy of IoT and Smart Cities will be more democracy. As another of the book's "Essential Truths" states, we must make the difficult transition from hoarding data, as we did in the past, to sharing it for mutual benefit.

With this in mind, whoever does not want to join this revolution always has the option to live in a house in the mountains, without risks, without worries and, of course, without the internet. The rest of the people must read this book!

—Alicia Asín,
co-founder and CEO of Libelium, Zaragoza, Spain

PREFACE

The Internet of Things is primarily about "stuff"—material things—especially as it is increasingly merged with the digital. However, I think it's equally about a fundamental shift in how we view and manage the world around us: learning things we never even saw about the material world, let alone understood, and then improving on them.

I wrote about the IoT for the first time around 2000, when the concept was referred to as "ubiquitous computing." I wrote about a nifty pipeline leak detection sensor that was self-powered by the pipeline's vibration. Think about a remote pipeline in the middle of nowhere developing metal fatigue, and repair crews pinpointing the problem and getting there in time to make repairs before there's a leak. A win-win for the company and the environment.

I returned to the concept with a brief passage in my 2011 book, *Data Dynamite*,[1] which argued that fully taking advantage of the Big Data explosion would require a paradigm shift from hoarding data to sharing it. That later became one of my four "Essential Truths" of the IoT (more about that in Chapter 2). I found the IoT concept fascinating and vowed to return to it after finishing the book.

I did that in late 2012, focusing my blog on the topic and writing an e-book, *SmartStuff*, on the concept. Then SAP selected me for a project, creating an e-guide to the IoT for C-level executives, *Managing the Internet of Things Revolution*.[2] Ultimately, that project led me to this book.

The other factor influencing the book was my work in the '90s to promote a concept I called "natural wealth," which sought to bring the 200+-year-old industrial economy into line with the 4.5-billion-year-old natural economy, which constantly evolves its "products," makes them out of locally available materials, assembles them at ambient temperatures, and makes productive use of its wastes. Until our recent attempts to muck things up, the natural economy has evolved pretty well.

Nature got me interested in cyclical processes, as opposed to the hierarchical and linear ones that are the hallmark of industry. In 1995, I wrote "The Buckyball Corporation" for *Network World*,[3] speculating that new internet-based software might allow us to form organizations resembling the "buckyball" molecule, in which every employee would be like a buckyball node, looking inward within a globe and able to see—and work with—every other person/node on the buckyball. A little on the fringe, but it did get me thinking about the benefits of abandoning hierarchy and linear processes: everyone able to work together, etc. Two decades later, it dawned on me that the truly revolutionary thing about the IoT wasn't cool devices that you could control from the other side of the world (as neat as that might be!) but the ability, for the first time, for everyone who needed real-time data about things and how they worked, to share that data instantly.

As you'll see, that could undermine the increasingly dysfunctional hierarchies and processes that still distinguish businesses, and lead to cyclical ones that would eliminate waste, encourage collaboration, and unleash the kind of creativity and innovation only possible when many participants from different backgrounds, responsibilities and insights work together!

In addition to my wife, Dr. Rebecca G. Stephenson, D.P.T., who has remained steadfast in support of my dogged efforts to build understanding of the IoT, I'm indebted to my agent, Jeff Herman, who interested HarperCollins Leadership. Editor Timothy Burgard provided invaluable insights, and copy editors Jeff Farr and Leigh Grossman, a sharp #2 pencil. Dear friend Bob Weisberg provided numerous ideas via Twitter, while constantly prodding me to meet my deadlines. I hope that I have made all of them proud.

INTRODUCTION

My acid test for innovation is a question posed by my friend Eric Bonabeau: "What can you do now that you couldn't do before?" That is, don't be content to just improve on the past, but fundamentally change it.

When I first learned about the Internet of Things (IoT), I realized that its most sweeping answer to Eric's question was that, for the first time, we could "see" inside things, from cows to massive machinery, learning exactly how they were operating (or not) right now. That in turn would eliminate our prior reliance on guessing, either wildly or perhaps on the basis of past performance. That led to inefficiency, "just-in-case" contingency spending, and slower improvements in products and their performance. As a result, my first focus for this book was on the unprecedented precision the IoT would allow, and the benefits that precision would produce:

- integrating supply chains, manufacturing, and distribution to an unprecedented degree
- replacing guesstimate-based scheduled maintenance with predictive maintenance, done at the first sign of a problem, with less cost and disruption and greater customer satisfaction

- speeding product upgrades that delight customers and build loyalty
- creating new revenue streams by marketing products as services.

However, what really seized my imagination, and what I believe is the ultimate example of "what can you do that you couldn't do before," was an inspiration that came to me after reading Heppelmann and Porter's second article on the IoT in the *Harvard Business Review*, when they predicted—but didn't specify how—the IoT could also fundamentally alter not just our products but how we manage the companies that make them:

> For companies grappling with the transition [to the IoT], organizational issues are now center stage—and there is no playbook. We are just beginning the process of rewriting the organization chart that has been in place for decades.[1]

It suddenly popped into my mind that a concept I'd been thinking of for more than twenty years—the possibility of *circular* management forms and processes replacing the linear and hierarchical ones that have dominated business since the birth of the Industrial Revolution—might be possible because of another aspect of the IoT obscured by our fascination with the new products and processes: for the first time, everyone who needs immediate access to realtime data about things can *share* (the verb is critical) access to that data. That will in turn allow removing data "silos," changing linear processes to circular ones, and unleashing unprecedented creativity by allowing people with differing expertise, interests, and responsibilities to collaborate.

The Future Is Smart will combine these two previously impossible innovations: revolutionary new products and production, and circular management processes to facilitate them.

Part I, The IoT Revolution, introduces the IoT, the essential attitudinal shifts to capitalize on it, and the tools to make it a reality. Chapter 1 will give an overview of the IoT's promise. Chapter 2 addresses a critical but little-discussed obstacle to full development of the IoT's potential: to paraphrase Einstein, you can't solve problems with the same thinking that created them. Really capitalizing on the IoT will require major management attitudinal changes, what I call the "Essential Truths." Unless you make security a priority, sharing data instead of hoarding it, turning linear processes to cyclical ones, and reinventing products, you can buy all the IoT tech you want without realizing its full benefits.

Chapter 3 will give a brief history of the IoT's evolution to date, and a nontechnical introduction to the many (and growing) number of technologies whose independent developments have coalesced to make the IoT possible.

Chapter 4 will dwell at length on one of those tools, the "Digital Twin," both because it is so critical and because it neatly epitomizes the IoT's most essential quality, the seamless merger of the physical and digital. Keep it in mind throughout any discussions of IoT strategy as a handy visual reference!

Part II introduces you to how the IoT is transforming businesses today. The getting-started section (Chapters 5 and 6) will excite you with detailed discussions of how IoT-based strategies really will let you do things you never could before. Chapter 5 should give any company confidence to launch an IoT initiative. It zeroes in on two companies that are well over a hundred years old, are so rooted in the Industrial Age that they still make locomotives, and yet are also in the IoT vanguard: GE and Siemens. If they can make the switch, so can you! Chapter 6 details how a wide range of companies, from tech firms to agribusiness to insurance, are already profiting from the IoT. You're bound to find a pioneer whose circumstances resemble yours. Then there are the startups that aren't encumbered by Industrial Age mind-sets that are creating entirely new IoT-based products. Do you hear me, Alexa?

Part III, After the Revolution, will describe corporate strategies for the soon-to-come era (perhaps within the next five years) when the IoT will be fully realized.

Chapter 7 will detail how comprehensive IoT strategies, based on the few companies that have already made the most major commitments and are already beginning to realize tangible benefits, will seamlessly interweave the IoT into manufacturing, design, supply chains, and distribution networks, and, after the sale, user experiences and maintenance.

Finally, Chapter 8 will describe my vision of how the IoT will not only transform our products and how we make and use them, but also sets the stage—because everyone who needs realtime data to do their job better will be able to *share* that data for the first time—for the first fundamental shift in corporate organization since the Industrial Age. The Circular Company will let us get rid of departmental information silos and work collaboratively with others, not only in the company but also with supply chain and distribution partners, and even with customers, with everyone sharing "ground truth." The result of having a whole range of people and departments batting around ideas and perspectives at the same time will be a continuous dialectic in which problems will be spotted early and dealt with efficiently, plus unprecedented creativity. It will lead to new products, services, and procedures that none of the participants could have created working in isolation. New developments such as "Scrum" and "Slack" show that the old linear processes aren't working. The IoT can lead to the solution.

PART I: **THE IoT REVOLUTION**

1

Profitably Close the Circle
with the IoT

"When wireless is perfectly applied, the whole earth will be converted into a huge brain, which in fact it is, all things being particles of a real and rhythmic whole."

—NIKOLA TESLA[1]

You'll never think of "things" and their changing impact on business the same way after learning about the BigBelly, a microcosm of the emerging Internet of Things.

Behold the traditional municipal trash can! What could be more primitive a thing?

Smelly.

Dented.

Overflowing with trash (and maybe rodents).

Often lying on its side.

And dumb—*really dumb*—it just sits there.

Unless, that is, the trash can is the BigBelly, a sleek, attractive, enclosed container whose solar electric-powered compacter lets it hold five times as much trash, paired with one or more recycling containers. These features alone would be a noteworthy advance compared to conventional municipal trash cans.

But the BigBelly Solar startup wasn't content to just improve the efficiency of trash and recyclable collection. In the early models, a red light turned on if the BigBelly was nearing its capacity. But with the emergence of the cloud, the company and Digi (a pioneer in the wireless Machine to Machine [M2M] communications field) added wireless communications to the bins, making them "smart." According to Marketing VP Leila Dillon, "We were there before there was an Internet of Things, connecting through the cloud. Our 'aha' moment was that we suddenly realized we could work with cities to transform their waste operations."[2]

Now, instead of traditional pickup routes and schedules probably based on sheer proximity (or, as BigBelly puts it a little more colorfully, "muscle memory and gut instincts"), the company offers a *realtime* way to monitor actual waste generation, through the wireless "CLEAN Management Console." That lets DPW personnel monitor and evaluate bins' fullness, trends, and historical analysis, for perspective. Collection schedules can now be dynamic and driven by what's happening *right now* rather than just past averages. On average, cities using BigBelly receptacles reduce the frequency of collections by 70 to 80 percent, while increasing the amount of materials that are recycled.

BigBelly Solar offers a Managed Services option where it analyzes the data and manages the devices on a subscription basis—not unlike the way jet turbine manufacturers and other companies now have substituted services for selling products, offering their customers value-added data that lets the customers optimize performance and generating new revenue streams for the manufacturers. The same communications network can even dramatically increase recycling programs' participation rates and efficiency.

That's not all.

Most recently, according to Dillon, the company has come to realize it has a "precious asset" because the units "are located exactly where the people are." Their engineering team began to think of a city's core needs and understood that the company could make better use of the wireless communications capability they already had. Given the rapid growth of IoT-based "smart city" services, they are now working with host cities to add services such as free Wi-Fi hot spots, IoT beacons to guide pedestrians, and sensors to detect ambient weather conditions. Because the BigBelly receptacles are just placed on location, rather than being built in, installation of new functions is easy and quick, with no wiring required. They can add sophisticated small-cell technology to deal with frequent bandwidth deficits and even bring Wi-Fi to underserved residential neighborhoods.

With BigBelly's decision to offer an open Application Programming Interface (API), smart people will be able to discover other uses for BigBelly data as well.

No wonder the company's website heralds BigBelly as "a platform deployed in the public right-of-way that delivers much more than smart waste and recycling. In addition to modernizing a core city service, it is optimal for hosting additional technologies. It is easy to access and can hide technology in plain sight."

Bottom line: If something as humble and ubiquitous as a municipal trash receptacle can be transformed into a waste-reduction-recycling collection-municipal communications hub, imagine what could happen if we reexamined *every* conventional product and management system and found ways to make them "smart" through the Internet of Things.

The Internet of Things (IoT), the concept that every "thing," ranging from assembly-line sensors to light bulbs to trees in remote rain forests and cows in a pasture, can be given a distinctive name and then be linked to other things via the internet or a local wired or wireless network, is what creates this ability to uncover and use previously inaccessible information about man-made and natural things. The Internet of Things lets manufacturers and others gather data from these devices, interpret it, and act on it, *all in realtime*—something that was impossible in the past, and that will change everything.[3] The benefits range from cheaper, quicker, and better maintenance to increased manufacturing efficiency, to product design that will delight customers and create new revenue streams.

But neat, efficient products and services just touch the surface of what the IoT can do if we realize the true significance of realtime data sharing among everyone who needs it.

Less understood (and a major theme of this book) is that the IoT can even let you abandon outmoded hierarchical and linear processes. It will enable a radically new circular management model that was impossible in an era of limited data, one that increases operating efficiency, sparks innovation, and promotes collaboration. That's because, for the first time, everyone in an organization who needs access to realtime data to make better decisions or do their job more efficiently can instantly *share* that data.

The Future Is Smart will provide the overview you need of the major technologies required to implement an IoT strategy, and detail the key areas such as manufacturing, maintenance, and design that it will change. Perhaps even more important, it will introduce you to the radical attitudinal shifts you must make to capitalize on the IoT's full potential to transform every aspect of your company and its thinking.

To better understand the IoT's potential, consider the following examples. You will notice, because they are based on accurate, realtime information never before available about how things actually work, they differ from past practices that had to work around information gaps and unconnected things. There's simply no comparison to business as usual in the past.

Car insurance companies in the past had to cobble together quotes based on proxy indicators such as credit reports ("guilty of driving while poor," in industry parlance) or teens' report cards. Progressive Insurance can now give you an accurate quote based on your actual driving behavior because it first sends you a "Snapshot" unit, which plugs into the diagnostic slot on your dashboard and monitors your driving for a month. If you're a safe driver, the Snapshot can earn you a discount. Insurers are extending the same approach to building insurance by monitoring realtime data on buildings' systems.

Kardia, a tiny metallic unit that fits on the back of your smartphone and costs less than a hundred dollars, will give an FDA-approved accurate EKG of your heart in only thirty seconds, comparable to a $10,000 inpatient procedure. If you want, it can automatically connect you with a cardiologist who can give a professional interpretation, via that smartphone. In fact, journal articles have shown Kardia's results can actually be more valuable than the costly inpatient variety because the readings are taken while you're active, rather than lying flat on your back in a hospital, and you can annotate them and share them instantly with your doctor. One cardiologist at the prestigious Massachusetts General Hospital now prescribes them for every patient.[4]

GE now builds fifty to sixty sensors into each of their jet engines. They use the realtime data from the sensors (a single 787 flight can produce a half a terabyte of data) to detect possible problems so early that the needed parts will be on hand and the engines can usually be fixed the next time the plane lands. That innovation is called "predictive maintenance," avoiding more costly emergency repairs and possible catastrophic crashes. Equally important as a demonstration of the IoT's truly transformative nature, both the manufacturer and the airlines benefit in other ways: If an airline opts in, GE will send them the realtime data, which can be combined with weather and other data streams to improve in-flight economy and performance, in return for a subscription fee that enhances the manufacturer's revenues. It's a far cry from the slapdash maintenance of the past.

In these and countless other examples, companies are able to make radical changes to every aspect of their operations based on the availability of unprecedented amounts of realtime data, while multiple users benefit from sharing the data.

The convergence of several technologies evolving over the past decade makes the Internet of Things possible:

- Cheap and low-powered sensors detect and then report, by wire or (increasingly) wirelessly, on a growing array of real-time factors, from babies' heartbeats to jet turbines' revolutions. There are now lithium-ion batteries the size of a grain of sand (created through another innovation, 3-D printing), and sensors as thin as a hair. A recent breakthrough will enable users to harvest ambient "backscatter" sound to power their devices—for free.

- Actuators act on that data without human intervention to fine-tune assembly lines and product operations.

- Changes in internet nomenclature make it possible to give distinctive internet addresses to countless things of all types— 3.4×10^{38} things, to be more precise—more than the total number of grains of sand on the earth.

- Billions of mobile devices provide a fertile environment—11.6 billion of them by 2020.[5]

- Expansion of cloud storage allows ready access to massive amounts of data, coupled with dramatic reductions in cloud storage's price—down to free in some cases.

- Development of sophisticated data analysis tools allows almost *realtime* analysis of the huge volume of data these sensors yield and the ability to visualize it in ways that laymen can understand.

Some have called the Internet of Things the Third Age of Computing (after mainframes and then personal computers and the internet). It promises to revolutionize *every* aspect of business in the next decade and help workers at every level of the enterprise. The Internet of Things will:

- Streamline and integrate supply chains, manufacturing, and distribution, because all parties will be able to instantly share realtime manufacturing data, so supply and distribution can be automated. This will result in an unprecedented degree of precision in all aspects of operations while reducing waste and inefficiency.

- Improve decision making, because you will no longer have to depend entirely on fragmentary historic data. Various departments can analyze and act on the data simultaneously, rather than sequentially.

- Create new revenue streams, by selling customers realtime data that will help them optimize operating efficiency. Many products may now be marketed instead as services, with mutual benefits to manufacturer and customer.

- Improve and speed product design, because you'll get real-time data on how customers actually use your products.

- Delight customers, by making innovations such as mass customization, Augmented Reality (AR), and 3-D printing practical. Customers may actually be the final step in the process, making personal choices that will dictate key aspects of how the product works.

Bear in mind that these are only the early-stage benefits before we make the more radical management changes that can lead to the Circular Company.

The Internet of Things' economic impact will be profound.

In 2013, when the IoT was just taking hold, it was estimated to produce $613 billion in global corporate profits just for industrial applications.[6] According to Juniper Research, the number of connected devices, sensors, and actuators will exceed $46 billion in 2021.[7] Research Nester predicted in 2017 that the market will reach $724.2 billion by 2023, with a compound annual growth rate (CAGR) globally of 13.2 percent from 2016 to 2023.[8]

General Electric has made a sweeping commitment to the IoT, using the marketing term "Industrial Internet" to describe its initiative. GE predicts that, "If the cost savings and efficiency gains of the Industrial Internet can boost U.S. productivity growth by 1 to 1.5 percentage points, the benefit in terms of economic growth could be substantial, potentially translating to a gain of 25 to 40 percent of current per capita GDP."[9] An entire chapter of this book will detail how GE and its European counterpart, Siemens (both major suppliers of IoT services), have proven their claims about the IoT's transformative potential by applying it to their own strategy and operations. Gartner now places the IoT at the height of its famous "hype cycle," and says it is "becoming a vibrant part of our customers' and our partners' business and IT landscape."[10]

While still mentioned only occasionally by mainstream media and still more a matter of research rather than active implementation by most major businesses, a growing number of both leading companies and startups are aggressively pursuing Internet of Things strategies.[11] These strategies are cutting operating costs, increasing revenues and efficiency, and delighting customers. In many cases, these companies are doing things that were *simply impossible* before the Internet of Things and its ability to understand and link things:

- A prototype vending machine created by SAP allows a snack food company to customize offers for individual consumers based on their past buying practices and lets those individuals pay electronically. Also, if a given machine runs low due to unforeseen circumstances such as a hot day at the beach, the same data would automatically be used—without requiring a human dispatcher—to reroute a delivery truck to restock the machine in time to avoid disappointed customers. This illustrates a key aspect of the IoT, that data can be shared in *realtime* by a wide range of users who might benefit from it in different ways, rather than having to pass it on sequentially.

- John Deere creates new revenue streams and satisfied customers with its FarmSight technology, which lets farmers plow precisely, with no overlap, and apply exactly the amount of fertilizer needed at just the right time. Deere used to build a variety of tractor engines for various requirements. Now it ships a standard engine and allows each user to choose what configuration to use through software.

- Electric car manufacturer Tesla faced a serious problem—a design issue that could result in a fire. The solution? Instead of mailing owners a notice and hope they would come in for an inconvenient and time-consuming recall, Tesla solved the problem with an automatic, overnight software update to *every* car.

- Startups such as Nest are reinventing old products such as thermostats and door locks, building in IoT capabilities to delight consumers while helping them save money. Others, such as Ambient Devices, create entirely new products such as the Orb, an attractive table ornament used for everything from cutting companies' electricity use to tracking stock prices.

- From the sublime to the perhaps ridiculous, a Lithuanian startup has created a women's shoe whose wearer can instantly change its appearance simply by touching a new pattern on a smartphone app, which produces that pattern in an insert on the side of the shoe.

These are only a few of a wide range of examples of how the Internet of Things is improving business processes and customer relations. The IoT will eventually change our fundamental relationship with products. They will "talk" to us, with sensors constantly monitoring their status and instantly reporting data to manufacturer and customer alike.

That realtime data will uncover a range of possibilities for products and processes that is impossible to visualize now, because the IoT lets us overcome a limit to our literal and figurative vision that I'll call "Collective Blindness."

COLLECTIVE BLINDNESS

It's hard to visualize in advance exactly how profound this transition will be, but we must try, because the real power of the Internet of Things doesn't come just from enabling technology, but also from learning to rethink the material world and how we relate to it because of this new information flow.

Technologist Jeffrey Conklin has written of "wicked problems" that are so complex they aren't even known or detailed until solutions to them are found.[12] What if there had been a wicked problem, a universal human malady that we'll call "Collective Blindness," whose symptoms were that we humans simply could not see much of what was happening in the material world? We could only see the surface of these things, while their interiors and actual operations were impenetrable to us. For millennia we just came up with coping mechanisms to work around the problem of not being able to peer inside things, which we accepted as reality.

Collective Blindness was a stupendous obstacle to full realization of a whole range of human activities. But, of course, we couldn't quantify the problem's impact because we weren't even aware that it existed.

In fact, Collective Blindness *has* been a reality, because vast areas of our daily reality have been unknowable and we have accepted those limits as a condition of reality.

For example, in a business context:

- We couldn't tell when a key piece of machinery was going to fail due to metal fatigue.

- We couldn't tell how efficiently an assembly line was operating or how to fully optimize its performance by having changes in one machine trigger adjustments in the next one.

- We couldn't tell whether or when a delivery truck would be stuck in traffic, or for how long.

- We couldn't tell exactly when we'd need a parts resupply shipment from a supplier. (Let's be honest: what we've called "just-in-time" in the past was hopelessly inexact compared to what we'll be able to do in the future.) Nor would the supplier know exactly when to do a new production run in order to be ready.

- We couldn't tell how customers actually used our products once they were in the field, or help those customers adjust operations to make them more efficient.

That's all changing now.

The wicked problem of Collective Blindness is ending, because the Internet of Things solves it, giving us realtime information about what's happening inside things. Remember, for example, that half a terabyte of data from a single jet turbine on a single flight!

The Internet of Things will affect and improve every aspect of business because it will allow us to eliminate all of those blind spots resulting from Collective Blindness, achieve efficiency, and derive insights that were impossible before.

Cisco, which focuses not only on the IoT's enabling technologies but also on the management issues it will address, understands the Collective Blindness concept. It refers to previously opaque and unconnected things as "dark assets," and says that, "The challenge is to know which dark assets (unconnected things) to light up (connect) and then capture, analyze, and use the data generated to improve efficiency while working smarter."[13]

PTC has created the most literal cure for Collective Blindness: Vuforia, an AR system that lets an operator or repair person wearing an AR headset to go from looking at the exterior of a Caterpillar power generator to "seeing" an exploded view of the system that shows each part and how they connect as well as monitoring the realtime performance data of each component, gathered by sensors on the machinery. That insight can also be shared, in realtime, by others who need it.

"A HUGE BRAIN"

Dramatic as they are, these examples pale by comparison with what experts predict will be possible when the Internet of Things becomes ubiquitous in the next few years—as the cost of components drops even more, the supporting infrastructure becomes more robust and cheaper, and perhaps most important, we begin to think differently. There are confident predictions of an end to traffic jams, user-customizable products—and seamless, precise supply-chain, manufacturing, and distribution cycles.

The "network effects" phenomenon will kick in.

That's Robert Metcalfe's concept that the value of any network is the square of the number of devices. The more IoT-connected devices there are and the easier it becomes to connect and integrate them seamlessly, the more valuable and helpful each device will become. As Brynjolfsson and McAfee have written in another context, this will allow "recombinant innovation," in which digital components are continually recombined in novel ways: "Possibilities do not merely add up, they multiply."[14] Network effects are already beginning, especially as manifested by the If This Then That site (IFTTT, http://ifttt.com), where various IoT devices and other sources are increasingly brought together by "recipes" in which an action such as a weather change or leaving your workplace triggers simultaneous actions by several devices.

When network effects are fully realized, the earth will in fact become the "huge brain" Tesla visualized in the quotation at the top of this chapter, "all things being particles of a real and rhythmic whole."[15] When that happens, we'll see that the rosy estimates for the IoT's economic impacts will prove to be conservative: we'll discover an infinite number of synergies between devices that will make each of them more powerful and efficient.

EVERY ASPECT OF BUSINESS WILL BENEFIT

You need to know about the Internet of Things now, not just when it becomes commonplace. That's because being able to base decisions on comprehensive, realtime information instead of just guesstimates and limited historical data will improve every aspect of business (each of these benefits will be explored in depth in later chapters):

- **Unprecedented assembly line precision and product quality.** Workers and management will have realtime data from the products themselves and from the assembly line. Unprecedented integration of the supply chain, the factory floor, and the distribution network will result, because it will be possible—if management chooses to allow it—for all of these workers and functions to simultaneously share realtime data about what is happening on the assembly line.

- **Drastically lower maintenance costs and product failure.** It will be possible to "see" inside products and detect issues such as material fatigue. Predictive maintenance will occur long before a product fails or requires an emergency repair, and that information will be fed back into the design process to modify products so the same problems won't reoccur. As one wag said, "Why schedule a train's maintenance, when the train can do it itself."

- **Increased customer delight and loyalty.** Products will be designed to give customers opportunities to customize them through software configurations instead of hardware, and to update them through software upgrades instead of requiring complete replacements.

- **Improved decision making.** This will happen both within the organization and with important contributors such as supply-chain and distribution partners (and perhaps even directly involving customers) because it will be possible for everyone who needs realtime data about devices' status to share it and do so instantly. This will break down information silos within a company and promote continuous collaboration between functions such as product design, manufacturing, and marketing whose decisions have always affected each other in the past but have worked in isolation from each other, reducing efficiency and robbing one department of the other's insights.

- **Creating new business models and revenue streams.** Instead of ending their relationship with customers when the product goes out the door, manufacturers will increasingly shift from just selling products to providing services to customers— to helping customers to use their products more efficiently, economically, and safely. In the process, manufacturers will create new revenue streams for themselves.

- **Revolutionizing management.** Our current management styles, hierarchical and linear, were logical coping mechanisms in the day when it was difficult to collect data about things and operations and equally hard to share it. Management decided which information to give to who, and when.

Most dramatically, these factors will combine so we can move to new circular management structures linking all parts of the enterprise—its suppliers, distribution network, and customers—in a continuous loop with realtime data as the hub. It's impossible to overstate what a fundamental transformation the Internet of Things will ignite for business because of this shift of making previously inscrutable things visible and understandable.

As one analysis by a European study group put it, "Imagine things having identities and virtual personalities operating in smart spaces using intelligent interfaces to connect and communicate within social, environmental, and user contexts."[16]

Yes, imagine what that would mean!

It will take both new technology *and*, equally important, a major shift in our attitudes to think more expansively and fully capitalize on this newfound information.

It's impossible to predict what the improvements will be once we end Blindness. Only when the data streams begin to flow, as previously "dumb" devices report their status, as they communicate with other devices, and as they even control each other, will we be able to interpret and act on that data. Only then will we begin to realize how devices that we thought of as independent and isolated from each other can actually interact and increase each other's utility, and that we can and must organize our enterprises around that data.

MOST COMPANIES DON'T HAVE
IoT STRATEGIES

While leaders such as GE, John Deere, and Union Pacific are already reinventing their businesses using the Internet of Things, the reality is that most companies haven't even begun to create an IoT strategy. Few have begun to realize the low-hanging-fruit benefits that can be realized right now by optimizing a variety of current operations and employing early-stage IoT technologies—not to mention the total transformations possible when they are fully realized.

A 2014 study by Capgemini Consulting, *The Internet of Things: Are Organizations Ready for a Multi-Trillion Dollar Prize?*, reported that 42 percent of the companies it surveyed had not created any IoT services. The report concluded with an ominous warning to those who are holding back:

> The IoT represents the next evolution of the digital universe. The speed at which nimble startups and Internet players are capturing IoT opportunities should serve as a wake-up call to larger, traditional organizations. Analyst estimates point to a world where startups will dominate the IoT market. Fifty percent of IoT solutions are now expected to originate in startups less than three years old. They may be less nimble, but bigger organizations need to step up to the plate. As with all digital disruptions, being an organization that is in catch-up mode will be a deeply uncomfortable place to be.[17]

ENJOY THE IoT'S BENEFITS—
DON'T BE A VICTIM

The Future Is Smart was written to help companies avoid being marginalized by the Internet of Things, and instead enjoy its benefits. It will help you personally to identify new career opportunities and realize how to add relevant new skills and attitudes to capitalize on this revolution.

You will learn the basics of the essential technology that makes the IoT possible, and how to implement today's early versions of those devices to optimize your current operations. Even without fundamental changes such as redesigning products to include sensors, you will reduce waste and inefficiency and amortize your prior investments in predictive analytics and other big data tools and infrastructure.

However, something as transformational as the IoT will require more than just new technology. It will also require fundamental changes in management practices—and perhaps more important, in management attitudes—to capitalize on this new ability to learn about and harness things creatively. For example, in the past, management exercised tight, hierarchical access to data, in part because this information couldn't be shared simultaneously due to technology limits: it was committed to paper and edited. Only then did managers pass along what *they* deemed to be relevant information to those who *they* decided needed it. No wonder managers were so powerful.

Now those limits will be eliminated. It will be feasible *to share simultaneous, realtime access* to information with absolutely *everyone* who needs it to work more efficiently: your entire workforce, your supply chain, your distribution network, and perhaps even your customers. But will managers be willing to give up their control of data and its use? How will they restructure reporting and decision making? Will they abandon traditional hierarchies?

BEGIN THE TRANSFORMATION

The price, size, and energy supplies of IoT components must still be reduced before the IoT will become ubiquitous and realize its full potential for change. Nevertheless, smart companies such as GE and John Deere are gaining a competitive advantage today through lower operating costs and greater efficiency, while creating new revenue streams, by taking the lead in transforming themselves into IoT companies now.

SELF-ASSESSMENT

1. Were you handicapped in the past by inability to know, in realtime, how your products actually operate in the field? Did that increase your costs, especially for maintenance? Did it slow the upgrade process?

2. What benefits do you think you'll get from being able to obtain and share this data in realtime?

3. Do you know what your company's IoT privacy and security practices are? Are they robust? Iterative? Is your company part of any industrywide consortium working on IoT strategy?

4. Is your company still hoarding data, keeping it from your supply chain, distribution network, or customers? Have you launched specific initiatives to share this data? What benefits do you think you'll receive from sharing data?

5. Have your company's processes been linear in the past? Are you now moving to circular ones? What benefits do you expect to receive?

6. Are you planning to rethink your products and their role in your company? Will you be substituting services for the sale of products? Will this increase customer satisfaction?

2

··

Essential Truths

Remember the stories about executives in the mid-nineties who'd started using that newfangled tool called "email"? They'd have their secretaries print the emails out and put them in a neat pile on their desk.

True or not, there was an important moral to the story: You can adopt all the new IoT tools you can afford, but if you don't make significant attitudinal changes to capitalize on them, you won't be able to exploit the IoT's full potential. Those entrenched attitudes from the past will interfere with fundamental aspects of the IoT. Hampered by them, you may be oblivious to the potential for change because your blinders won't even let you see them.

In the case of the IoT, there are four of these attitudes—let's call them "Essential Truths":

1. Privacy and security must be top priority.
2. Share data, don't hoard it.

3. Close the loop.

4. Rethink products—and their roles.

As you will see, they are complementary and synergistic, so that adopting several or all produces cumulative benefits that are far greater than each would have produced by itself.

[ESSENTIAL TRUTH #1]
PRIVACY AND SECURITY MUST BE TOP PRIORITY

Time for some tough love.

No matter how cool your IoT device or service is, if you're not willing to make guaranteeing privacy and security your top priority, you don't deserve to be in the field.

But isn't that putting the cart before the horse? Shouldn't you concentrate on creating your neat device first, then bolt on some privacy and security protections?

That's what I heard while speaking at a conference on wearables several years ago. When asked about their privacy and security protections, the bright-eyed duo who were presenting begged off: "We're just a startup—we'll get to the privacy and security when we have a workable prototype."

Nope. You don't have that luxury.

Consumer and Corporate Confidence
Is Hard to Win and Easy to Lose

Here's why.

Back in the eighties, I was a corporate crisis consultant, called in to rebuild public confidence after major companies had done something really dumb.

Customers' loss of confidence usually manifested itself as fear. The engineers with whom I'd work were usually dismissive of these fears, because they weren't fact-based, and I had to patiently explain that just because they weren't factual didn't mean they weren't very real in the customers' minds—and that those customers wouldn't be coming back soon.

That's even more the case with the IoT. Whether it's dealing with consumers or corporate customers, the kinds of realtime data that the IoT is gathering, from personal medical conditions to assembly-line operations, is crucial to them. Let a bad guy get hold of it due to lax privacy or security protections, and not only will your IoT product or service be cooked, but you're also putting the entire concept at risk. The public and business customers alike may paint the Internet of Things with a broad brush and say "no thanks."

I'm not talking hypotheticals here. There have already been several high-profile breeches of IoT security that have gotten a lot of media coverage.

One was staged by a willing *Wired* reporter and two white-hat hackers, who tunneled into his Jeep's entertainment system. (This underscores, by the way, the fact that one of the IoT's prime attributes, that individual IoT devices become more valuable and versatile when they are linked, is also a major potential problem. Hackers can reach the most critical system, in this case the car's drivetrain, through another device.) They then proceeded to take over the controls, ultimately killing the engine while he was driving sixty miles per hour on an interstate.[1]

Or, frightening to any parent, several years ago a Houston couple heard a loud voice coming from their two-year-old's bedroom. When the father entered the room, he heard a man with an Eastern European accent making lewd remarks to his (thankfully) sleeping (and deaf) girl—the hacker had taken over her baby monitor. The father had taken precautions such as putting a password on the monitor, but the Hong Kong–based manufacturer had taken shortcuts with the device's security provisions, which ironically touted that it could be remotely monitored from anywhere in the world.[2]

Most frightening of all, because of its implications for widespread internet chaos, was an October 2016 distributed denial of service (DDoS) attack on a New Hampshire–based hosting firm. It temporarily made large portions of the internet unavailable in the U.S. and Europe.[3] The hackers had used the "Mirai" malware to infect a wide range of cheap IoT devices, including printers, IP cameras, and baby monitors that had few protections (i.e., passwords such as "admin") or none at all. Can you imagine, five years in the future, if a similar attack was launched again, only this time taking over billions of IoT devices as the IoT multiplies?

These and other IoT privacy and security incidents illustrate that the very principle that makes the IoT so versatile and powerful, the fact that a variety of devices can be linked, means that an attack on one of the devices can potentially affect all of them. That's an argument for not just making privacy and security the highest priority with your own devices, but also for joining in collaborative efforts to reduce risk, as will be detailed later in this chapter.

Shodan

The extent of the IoT's vulnerability is demonstrated by Shodan, which bills itself as "the search engine for the Internet of Things." Some have called it "the scariest search engine on the Internet."[4]

Shodan capitalizes on an aspect of web structure that lets it use a variety of filters to query IP addresses (remember that IP addresses for almost every "thing" is a key tool for the IoT) for a whole range of devices, from routers to webcams: "The feed includes images of marijuana plantations, back rooms of banks, children, kitchens, living rooms, garages, front gardens, back gardens, ski slopes, swimming pools, colleges and schools, laboratories, and cash register cameras in retail stores, according to Dan Tentler, a security researcher who has spent several years investigating webcam security. . . . 'It's all over the place,' he told *Ars Technica UK*. 'Practically everything you can think of.'"

Visitors to the site can query keywords to find the indexed devices and, sometimes, information such as default passwords. It can't be stressed enough: DDoS attacks based on infecting IoT devices such as these with malware have potential impacts far beyond the individual users:

If consumers were making an informed decision and that informed decision affected no one but themselves, perhaps we could let the matter rest. But neither of those conditions are true. Most consumers fail to appreciate the consequences of purchasing insecure IoT devices. Worse, such a quantity of insecure devices makes the internet less secure for everyone. What botnet will use vulnerable webcams to launch DDoS attacks? What malware will use insecure webcams to infect smart homes? When 2008-era malware like Conficker B affects police body cams in 2015, it threatens not just the reliability of recorded police activity but also serves as a transmission vector to attack other devices. "The bigger picture here is not just personal privacy, but the security of IoT devices," security researcher Scott Erven told *Ars Technica UK*. "As we expand that connectivity, when we get into systems that affect public safety and human life medical devices, the automotive space, critical infrastructure—the consequences of failure are higher than something as shocking as a Shodan webcam peering into the baby's crib."[5]

Security by Design

Another IoT Essential Truth to be discussed later in this chapter is "close the loop," instead of using traditional linear processes. The privacy and security issue forces us to deal with that concept here as well.

No matter how elegant your privacy and security measures are today, you simply can't rest: the process must be iterative and never-ending, because the threat from hackers is constantly changing. There's a growing consensus in both IoT companies and government regulators that what's needed is "security by design."[6] Security needs to be an integral part of the device's design from the beginning, followed by an iterative process to make sure it still works as challenges evolve.

Privacy and Data Protection by Design

The EU recognizes privacy as a fundamental human right, so Europe is much further along on this concept than the U.S. is (although the concept was endorsed by former FTC Chair Edith Ramirez and the Department of Homeland Security).[7] The EU has created an excellent overview, *Privacy and Data Protection by Design—from Policy to Engineering*, which is perhaps the best place to begin to develop security by design strategies.[8] In it, the authors first give a stark assessment of current privacy and security protections (or lack thereof) in IoT products and services:

> We observed that privacy and data protection features are, on the whole, ignored by traditional engineering approaches when implementing the desired functionality. This ignorance is caused and supported by limitations of awareness and understanding of developers and data controllers as well as lacking tools to realize privacy by design.[9]

The report goes on to argue for integrating technical solutions and addressing organizational procedures and business models as well, a great approach so that privacy and security and technology will reinforce each other rather than be at loggerheads. It also tells legislators and regulators that they must play an active role, so that any regulations or standards don't limit future innovation.

It gives an overview of what are lumped under the term "Privacy-Enhancing Technologies" (PETs), such as encryption, protocols for anonymous communications, attribute-based credentials, and private search of databases. It goes on to link these tools and overall design strategies to a company's legal obligations to protect privacy to design strategies. That makes it easy for the developer to choose technologies that will meet the requirements. It also cautions developers about the approach's current limits—both inherent limits and those due to the current early stages of strategies and technologies.

The report concludes with recommendations on how to overcome and mitigate those limits, and with a caveat: "Privacy by design is a technical approach to a social problem."[10] In other words, it can't be the entire answer.

Ensuring IoT privacy and security will only become more important—and risky—as IoT devices and services become more ubiquitous in the next few years. You will need to make it a central consideration in everything you do on the IoT and go beyond your own policies to also become active in collaborative IoT industry privacy and security initiatives, such as the IoT Security Foundation and BuildItSecure.ly,[11] because the collaborative nature of the IoT requires equally collaborative privacy and security approaches and because a scandal involving any company in the field threatens public confidence in the concept in general.

It will also be necessary for companies to work with government agencies to craft regulations that will, on one hand, root out the bad actors who jeopardize everyone's credibility and, on the other, avoid the kind of prescriptive government regulations that would inhibit IoT innovation. It remains to be seen what the Trump administration may do in this area, but the FTC during the Obama administration launched an admirable collaborative regulatory development process with the industry.[12]

SHARE DATA, DON'T HOARD IT

Don't get cocky because you think you've internalized the need to make privacy and security the top priority for your IoT projects. The second Essential Truth also represents a tremendous attitudinal challenge. It asks us to abandon a belief that's been ingrained in business strategy since the very birth of the Industrial Age: today, we must *share* data, not hoard it.

Let's go back a while: to 1789, to be exact. At that time, it was illegal to take plans for one of the revolutionary Arkwright spinning mills out of England because they gave the country such an economic advantage. However, no one could keep twenty-one-year-old mill mechanic Sam Slater from memorizing the plans, then booking passage to the United States, pretending to be a farm laborer, since it was also illegal for a skilled mechanic to emigrate. There he launched the U.S. Industrial Revolution by building a mill in Pawtucket, Rhode Island.

The same zero-sum mentality toward information, in which you were a winner if you possessed proprietary knowledge and I was a loser if I didn't, continues to shape our business strategies. Those of us in New England remember the brief "Massachusetts Miracle" of the 1980s, when a rash of companies flourished temporarily by building now-forgotten minicomputers with proprietary operating systems that cleverly kept customers dependent on them. Until, that is, open systems and PCs doomed them.

With the IoT, by contrast, it can be mutually advantageous to share the realtime data about things that the IoT produces. It's a variation on the "network effects" phenomenon that Ethernet inventor Robert Metcalfe discovered: a product or service's value increases proportionally to the number of users it has.

Indeed, a corollary to "share data, not hoard it" is that *we must learn to routinely ask: who else can use this data?*

For example, Pratt & Whitney now gathers as much as ten gigabytes of data *per second* from the five thousand sensors on its new jet turbines, which they use to detect the earliest sign of operating problems so they can do less expensive, more rapid "predictive maintenance."[13] But there's more: They also offer that data to their airline customers for a fee, creating a major new revenue stream while helping their clients. AirAsia Group, for example, saves up to $10 million in fuel costs yearly using that data to change flight paths and optimize air traffic flow.[14]

Sometimes the benefits of sharing IoT data are realized entirely within your company. SAP created a nifty prototype IoT snack vending machine that recognizes users who opt in by name when they approach using Near-Field Communication (NFC).[15] Then it asks, for example, if they "want the usual," based on past purchases. It might even offer a package discount for chips and a drink, as well as nutritional information.

That alone would be innovative, but the software firm goes further. Realtime data on the machine's remaining inventory is sent to the distribution warehouse, where machine-to-machine (M2M) processing updates what the driver will deliver to replenish the machine. If the overall system detects that one of the machines is experiencing especially high demand, then the driver's iPad will reroute her to that machine—all without human intervention.[16]

Data sharing in this way contributes to one of the IoT's most important business benefits: letting you squeeze out inefficiencies and operate with maximum precision. Continually analyzing the operating data and identifying deviations will allow you to make continuing, sometimes minute, adjustments to processes.

Perhaps the most widespread example of mutual benefits from sharing IoT data is the IFTTT (If This, Then That) site, where a constantly growing number of IoT device manufacturers post the Application Programming Interfaces (API) for their devices. Users—including those without any technical skills—can use the APIs to mash up various devices and commands. For instance, when it's time for bed, you say, "Alexa, trigger bedtime," and Amazon's Alexa will turn off the WeMo switches—two different devices from two different companies, linked into a powerful combination that makes both more versatile, created by a user who just wants to make his life easier!

Perhaps most striking is how a company sharing its IoT data instead of hoarding it can lead to benefits of a totally different kind. According to Chris Rezendes of IoTImpactLab, Grundfos, the Danish pump manufacturer, now builds sensors into the pumps it installs on remote water wells all over rural Africa, so that it is notified when a pump isn't working and needs servicing (since it can take days for a repairperson to reach there). Grundfos also made that data publicly available, and an ingenious local resident created a phone app that the women from villages miles from the wells can check before they leave with heavy water containers on their shoulders, to avoid a wasted trip if the pump isn't working.

Incidentally, that's a great example of a phenomenon that kicks in when you throw open access to IoT data. No matter how smart Grundfos's engineers in faraway Bjerringbro are, there's no way they would have invented this app: their work and life experiences are too different from the villagers'. Opening up data can harness the insights and needs of many users.

Perhaps the best ways for companies to begin testing the benefits of sharing data instead of hoarding it are in two areas of enlightened self-interest that serve both public and corporate needs: participating in collaborative "smart city" and IoT-based transportation initiatives. They will make your host community a more attractive and efficient place to do business and speed the flow of your corporate deliveries and commuting workers.

Smart cities (i.e., ones that use a wide range of realtime data collection sources to better and more economically manage their operations and resources and provide more value to constituents) are increasingly feasible, effective, and less expensive due to the willingness to share realtime data for the common good.

In the past, municipalities were handicapped. It was up to them, and the limited taxes and revenues they depended on, to fund infrastructure projects. Today, individuals, companies, and government all contribute to the mix, sharing their data. Often this is a side effect of investing in smart devices for their own needs.

- Asthma sufferers become *de facto* Health Department investigators just by taking a puff on their Propeller smart inhalers (if they opt in). Built-in GPS units notify the DPH exactly where they were when they suffered the attack, so it can identify and remedy asthma "hot spots."[17]

- Drivers become auxiliary traffic control officers in cities that negotiate contracts with Waze. When they report double-parkers or accidents, the traffic department and police are automatically notified, dramatically cutting response times.[18]

- Columbus, which won the Obama administration's "Smart Cities" competition in 2016, is working with commercial truckers on strategies such as realtime scheduling of down-town deliveries to reduce congestion and an interstate truck "platooning" system that will connect long-haul trucks on the region's interstates, speeding their arrival and reducing emissions.[19]

The "Things Network," a grassroots global initiative, is one of the most appealing smart cities initiatives, because it is designed not just to improve city services but also to turn the entire city into an IoT laboratory for free use and mutual benefit by city agencies, companies, and residents.[20] It was launched in July 2015 by an audacious group of ten Amsterdam technology activists, with no governmental mandate or support. In less than a month, and at a total cost of under $10,000, it created a free citywide IoT data network using only ten LoRaWAN gateways located throughout the city. Other residents quickly capitalized on the network, launching novel IoT initiatives such as one particularly suited to Amsterdam: an emergency alert system using sensors in canal boats' hulls, to alert owners that they were taking on water, so the boats could be saved. The group then launched a KickStarter campaign to create even cheaper LoRaWAN gateways (€300 each) and an effort to spawn similar networks worldwide.

As of the time of this writing, there are either Things Networks or efforts to create them in hundreds of cities and towns worldwide.

Equally important regarding the attitude shifts to sharing data needed to really capitalize on the IoT's promise is senior management's policies on data sharing within companies themselves.

Back in the days of almost no data gathering on operations and equal difficulty in sharing it, it made sense for senior management to parcel out data when and where they saw fit, with information typically being distributed in a linear fashion, so one department would deal with it and then hand it on, along with their edits and additions, to the next department. Because almost all of the data was historical, it was of little value in optimizing operations. The very small amount of operating data was usually collected by a low-level employee who would record readings from a few electro-mechanical gauges on a scheduled basis. Supervisors probably checked the records only in cases when the readings were significantly outside acceptable ranges. It was impossible to "ride the dials," making minute adjustments to fine-tune operations.

Today, by contrast, the IoT allows the instant gathering and sharing of realtime data, not only from assembly lines, but also supply chains, distribution networks, and even customers in the field. This allows the astounding 99.9985 percent quality rate at Siemens's Amburg "Factory of the Future"—*but only if senior management allows realtime access to everyone who needs it*, no matter what level of operations they represent.

The choice is yours.

CLOSE THE LOOP

It used to be that you'd push the last washing machine straight off the assembly line onto the truck, close the door, and then lose all contact with it and the eventual owner until she bought a new one—or called complaining about a broken part. You really didn't have any idea about how your products worked (or didn't) once they were sold and went into use. That Collective Blindness analogy mentioned earlier is an apt description of the problem.

What little feedback you did receive from customers probably skewed your perceptions. Because it was so difficult to communicate with you, those who really loved or really hated the product and therefore were motivated enough to contact you were overrepresented. What about those in the middle, who probably represented the vast majority of customers? Even worse, the limited information you did get was anecdotal, not specific data on the product's operations.

Communication was one-way, extremely limited, and linear.

The third critical attitudinal shift to fully capitalize on the IoT, closing the loop, is closely related to the second one and directly addresses that problem: not only do you need to share the data with everyone who needs it to make better decisions or to do their jobs more efficiently, but you must change policies and procedures to make certain that the data flows in cyclical fashion, not linear.

Cyclical data flows will help you get fast, accurate feedback on how your products really work. They will facilitate upgrades and immediately improve operations through tools such as automatic M2M controls that don't require human intervention.

That's a long way from the linear, industrial past.

Nothing capsulized that era better than Henry Ford's behemoth 1.6-x-1-mile River Rouge plant: Iron ore came in one end. Finished cars came out the other. The entire plant would be idled frequently when a critical part wasn't resupplied in time, and those at one end of the process had little idea what those at the other end were doing.[21]

By contrast, consider GE's Durathon battery factory in Schenectady (which the company shut down when it got out of the battery business in 2016—a reminder that the IoT will have its share of false starts before achieving maturity. The example is still relevant because of the IoT-based innovations it pioneered that can be copied elsewhere). GE put sensors in the Durathon batteries to monitor their condition in the field, similar to the sensors on the Grundfos water pumps mentioned earlier in this chapter, because the massive batteries were used as backup power for cell towers that might have been as remote as the water pumps. It could take days for a repairperson to reach them so owners needed to know as soon as possible about impending problems.[22]

Rather than tacking on the sensors at the end of production, GE built them in at the beginning. That provided another variation on sharing the data: in this case, the sensors didn't just report the batteries' operating status in the field, but also the status of the complex chemical reaction that produced them in the factory. Instead of product-testing practices dictated by the lack of real-time data (such as plucking every xth product off the assembly line and testing it), GE could monitor *every* battery throughout the entire production process, remove defective ones, and be certain that each one that completed the chemical process works.

The factory is closed, but the lessons are still inspiring.

The continuous circular data flow changes how we design things, how we manufacture them, how we service them, and even how we market them: all because we have a continuous data loop for the first time. Consider these benefits:

- **Product design.** "G.E. is adopting practices like releasing stripped-down products quickly, monitoring usage, and rapidly changing designs depending on how things are used by customers. These approaches follow the 'lean startup' style at many software-intensive Internet companies. 'We're getting these offerings done in three, six, nine months,' [William Ruh, the company VP of Global Software] said. 'It used to take three years.'"[23] Caterpillar's design process is refined because, for the first time, it knows how its heavy equipment is actually being used in the field.[24]

- **Precision manufacturing.** A major reason Siemens achieves 99.9985 percent quality at its "Factory of the Future" is that the real factory is paralleled by a "smart factory digital twin: representing a production system . . . which is completely connected to the main PLM [Siemens's proprietary software] data repository via sensors, SCADA systems, PLCs and other automation devices. In such a smart factory, all the events happening on the shop floor during production are recorded and the relevant ones are pushed back to the PLM system either directly or through the cloud."[25]

- **Predictive maintenance.** Instead of doing scheduled maintenance as in the past, in which maintenance intervals were as much guesstimate as science, with the IoT, maintenance is dictated by the product's actual status. The repair is scheduled at the first sign of an issue, before it becomes acute. Because of the realtime data from actual operations, the mechanic knows in advance what the problem is (imagine how much time and testing is required to diagnose a problem if the machine is turned off to protect the mechanic) and the replacement parts are already delivered by the time it enters the repair facility.

- **Selling services instead of products.** Because of the incredible amount of data that jet engines send to the ground, the turbine manufacturers have been emboldened to switch to a totally new marketing strategy. GE, with its "OnPoint" program, doesn't sell the engines but leases them, with the airline's cost determined by how much thrust they generate. That means if they're sitting in the repair facility they aren't generating revenue, so the manufacturers have a powerful incentive to make the repairs as quickly and cheaply as possible. Even better, as mentioned previously, the turbine manufacturers have created new revenue streams: airlines can pay an additional fee to get access to the flight data, which they can mash up with variables such as weather data and fuel prices to maximize their planes' flying efficiency.

We will discuss all of these advantages at length later in the book.

It's not hard to imagine a day in the near future when companies realize that maximizing precision requires sharing that realtime data with their supply chains, distribution networks, and customers, and that such a continuous data loop will mean just-in-time resupplying and distribution. Customers (if they opt in) may get realtime suggestions on how to fine-tune their equipment's operations for maximum efficiency and minimum operating costs.

RETHINK PRODUCTS AND THEIR ROLES

The jet turbine companies' switch to leasing is a great example of the fourth, and interrelated, IoT Essential Truth: rethink products and their roles. Because the manufacturer no longer needs to guess about whether the customer likes the product and how it's being used, product design and refinement becomes a continuous process, so that GE and others can now push a product upgrade out the door more rapidly and increase the chance that customers will be satisfied.

Software now becomes a key component of products, especially in terms of maintenance and upgrades. Tesla's response after a product recall because of issues with its suspension is a great example.[26] As *Wired* recounts:

"Not to worry," said Tesla, and completed the fix for its 29,222 vehicle owners via software update. What's more, this wasn't the first time Tesla has used such updates to enhance the performance of its cars. Last year it changed the suspension settings to give the car more clearance at high speeds, due to issues that had surfaced in certain collisions.[27]

Even better, the upgrade was done automatically, overnight, without requiring customers to go to a dealer.

Changing our attitudes about products can mean exciting breakthroughs that were unimaginable in the recent past. Consider the example of BigBelly trash bins in Chapter 1 and how they reinvented a traditionally mundane product. Also, because of designers capitalizing on the IoT's disruptive power, products that once were costly and so large that they had to be located in a permanent facility are now affordable and can fit in a pocket.

PUTTING THE ESSENTIAL TRUTHS TO WORK

Don't minimize the difficulty you'll face in scuttling old attitudes such as linear processes that we've inherited from the nineteenth-century Industrial Age. They're so ingrained in our subconscious that we're not even aware how much they shape our thinking and restrict our vision and our ability to consider alternatives. However, abandon them we must, because we'll never realize the IoT's full potential for customer satisfaction, production precision, and new revenue streams if we don't embrace the new attitudes—the Essential Truths—that the IoT entails.

SELF-ASSESSMENT

1. Does your company have a chief of security or a security officer? Does the security officer have any power over corporate policies, or is this mainly a technical and compliance role?

2. Are your privacy and security policies iterative, or are they only rarely upgraded?

3. If you are already creating IoT products or services, are privacy and security priorities from the beginning, or added on at the end?

4. Is your company involved in any collaborative industry-wide privacy and security organizations?

5. Is your corporate data tightly controlled by senior management? Do others have access to it only on a need-to-know basis?

6. Do you routinely ask, "Who else can benefit from sharing this data?" Is your default position to share data or to hoard it?

7. If you are making IoT devices, do you increase their value by sharing their APIs with IFTTT?

8. Do you participate in any IoT-based public-private smart city or transportation projects?

9. Do you routinely map your processes to see if they are linear and terminate in a dead end? Can you revamp them so they are circular and feed back realtime data

that can be used to fine-tune the process or enable M2M self-regulation?

10. Do you use digital twins to mirror products' or services' in-the-field status in the office? How have you used this data to create product enhancements or switch to predictive maintenance?

11. Have you considered whether the IoT might enable you to market products as services and create new revenue streams?

3

"Computers . . . Vanish into the Background"

Visionaries have written about the possibility of something akin to the IoT for years.

As Jay Nash put it in 1932, "Mechanical slaves . . . start our car; run our motors; shine our shoes." The two-way wrist radio made its first appearance in a 1946 *Dick Tracy* comic strip—and that fanciful device's importance can't be underestimated as a stimulus to the imaginations of many school-age would-be engineers for many years to come.[1]

Most agree that the most prophetic and accurate vision of the IoT was a 1991 *Scientific American* article by Xerox PARC scientist Mark Weiser about what he called "ubiquitous computing." He summed it all up in the first sentence: "The most profound technologies are those that disappear. They weave themselves into the fabric of everyday life until they are indistinguishable from it."[2]

Bingo!

Weiser went on to paint a vision of a day when computers themselves would "vanish into the background." He compared what would happen with computing to what had happened around the turn of the twentieth century, with the switch from a single motor that controlled all the devices in the house through a complex system of belts and pulleys to individual, increasingly small motors in each device. Similarly:

> Most of the computers that participate in embodied virtuality will be invisible in fact as well as in metaphor. Already computers in light switches, thermostats, stereos, and ovens help to activate the world. These machines and more will be interconnected in a ubiquitous network.[3]

He detailed a number of similar devices, some of which are similar to IoT devices today, some of which never took off. Weiser concluded that "the real power of the concept comes not from any one of these devices; it emerges from the interaction of all of them. The hundreds of processors and displays are not a 'user interface' like a mouse and windows, just a pleasant and effective 'place' to get things done."

Mostly a dream in 1991.

Mostly a reality today.

THE PIONEERS

It's critical as we trace the IoT's evolution to remember that the digital and the physical used to be thought of in isolation from each other, with the exception perhaps of CAD-CAM software that was used on computers to design physical things. If anything, we focused on how the digital was replacing many physical objects (streaming music, for example), with almost a bias about physical things being relics of a bygone age, while the future was digital and intangible. What has happened in the past thirty years is that the line has progressively been blurred, as physical, tangible things have increasingly become linked to, and interact with, the digital. It is this marriage of the two, and its benefits, that is the essence of the IoT.

As for IoT devices themselves, there are many possible claimants to which was first.[4] It's worth mentioning several of these precursors, because they illustrate the breadth of devices that are now lumped under the IoT rubric. The devices include most of the important IoT categories: commercial, wearables, and industrial. That underscores the fact that these have all evolved to be important areas of our lives and work that were previously impossible to document and control, resulting in inefficiency and lack of information.

One important thread of IoT antecedents for commercial uses is interactive, scannable labels, which are still valuable tools for everything from inventory control to retail checkout. They can be traced to 1949, when a young engineer traced four lines in the sand of a Miami beach, leading to his 1952 patent for the first bar code. That led in turn to the universal product code (UPC), which made its supermarket debut on June 26, 1974. In 1999 the UPC eventually evolved into the MIT-developed radio-frequency identification (RFID) tag, a true IoT technology because it allowed linking objects through the internet. (Incidentally, RFID Auto-ID Center director Kevin Ashton gave the Internet of Things its name.)[5]

Another important category of IoT precursors is wearable devices, which evolved by taking advantage of new communications capabilities to report on people's medical conditions or to give them enhanced powers, without being tethered to devices or being forced to go to a hospital or other location to have functions and conditions monitored. The first, in 1955, reminds us that IoT devices can include the ridiculous as well as the sublime: Edward Thorp's wearable computer, an analog one the size of today's smartphones, designed specifically to predict how to win at roulette. In 1960, the wearable computer was matched by Morton Heilig's head-mounted display, foreshadowing today's smartphones and visual displays such as the ill-fated Google Glass.

Particularly noteworthy was Hubert Upton's 1967 invention combining the two: a wearable computer and glasses-mounted display, to help deaf people lip-read. As with later IoT devices such as iPads used to help autistic children communicate, or powered exoskeletons that can help paralyzed people walk again, wearable devices have always held the promise of enhancing human capabilities.[6] Transformers, anyone?

The final category of noteworthy IoT precursors dealt with machine-to-machine (M2M), the concept of machines communicating directly among themselves and even, in some cases, activating each other. M2M had its antecedents in sonar and radar, but really got its start in 1968 with two widely different inventions, radio tracking of wolves by the state of Minnesota, and the creation of Caller ID by Metretek founder Theodore Paraskevakos. He later advanced the M2M concept with smart meters that could be read remotely and which have made possible the "smart grid" for electricity.[7]

However, many believe the actual IoT *really* began with thirst for a cold Coke. A gang of grad students at Carnegie Mellon in the early 1980s put micro-switches on the Coke machine and connected them to the department's Digital PDP-10 so they could find out how many bottles were in the machine and whether they were cold.[8]

We've come a long way since then!

NECESSARY TECHNOLOGIES

The Internet of Things evolved in patchwork fashion from the complementary but unplanned convergence of enabling technologies that were originally developed for a wide range of purposes, then fortuitously came together—epitomizing the IoT's emphasis on sharing and collaboration.

That cumulative aspect is important, because it means that you don't have to make a major up-front investment in a full-fledged IoT system. You can begin investments in any of those contributing technologies individually and begin to realize bottom-line yields from each of them long before you may institute a comprehensive IoT strategy. As we will see, it also means the IoT can easily adapt to emerging and complementary tech, such as Artificial Intelligence (AI) and 3-D printing.

The rest of this chapter will give an overview of these components. It's important that, while strategists shouldn't clutter their minds with technical details, understanding IoT tools' roles and benefits can help you create strategies that will capitalize on their individual and collective capabilities. That's especially true of those that allow you to combine the physical and digital effectively for mutual benefit. The discussion is not meant to be exhaustive. For example, it doesn't deal with key underlying IoT components such as actuators and controllers but focuses instead on those tools that make the IoT different from past technologies and are an appropriate focus for strategic decisions.

Internet

The first and most critical component, without which the IoT would be impossible, was of course the internet itself, which grew out of the military's ARPANET when it adopted TCP/IP in 1983. The internet was more than just the enabling technology for wireless communication and processing: It also sparked the incredibly diverse run of innovations that cumulatively resulted in the IoT and so many other paradigm-shifting developments in the past forty years. In the case of the IoT, the internet allows linking devices everywhere, which dramatically increases the potential for wide-ranging uses.

It wasn't certain early in this decade that the internet would be up to the task of handling all of the additional traffic generated by the IoT because the supply of IP addresses using the existing IPv4 protocol was in danger of being exhausted. That threat was eliminated for the foreseeable future when the range of potential internet addresses was increased through release of Internet Protocol v. 6 (IPv6) in 2006. It allows internet addresses up to 128 bits long, which will make possible creation of up to 340,282,366,920,938,463,463,374,607,431,768,211,456 distinct IP addresses.

At the same time, it's important to remember that many IoT innovations don't require the internet. They rely instead on Bluetooth, RFID, NFC, or other short-range wireless technologies to communicate data.

Mobile Devices

Another key IoT driver is mobile devices. By 2020 there will be 6.1 *billion* smartphone users globally, surpassing the number of landlines for the first time.[9]

It can't be quantified, but the ubiquitous nature of smartphones, tablets, and even smartwatches also increases the number of apps and devices controlled by them, simply due to the creative copycat phenomenon: when bright (even nontechnical) people see an effective IoT device or app, it can motivate them to invent a device or service applying the same technology to a radically different need.

Because businesspeople carry their own phones or other consumer devices constantly, it also makes sense for those phones to be used to control commercial and industrial IoT processes, rather than going to the time and expense of creating a single-purpose device to use as a control. At the previously mentioned GE Durathon battery factory, plant managers walked around with iPads to monitor the critical chemical processes in realtime, and during a particularly severe weekend storm that could have ruined the battery creation process because of sudden atmospheric changes, the manager monitored the situation from his iPad at home and fine-tuned the HVAC operations to avoid a problem.[10]

Analytical Tools

Another critical technology developed for other reasons but also crucial to the IoT are the analytical tools needed to process the already vast quantities of "big data" that have been created in the past decade due to the explosion of data from non-IoT devices. Investing both in data analysis and the data scientists to oversee it should be your starting point for an eventual IoT initiative because data analysis is so crucial to effective IoT strategy. It's one thing to collect huge quantities of data from sensors, but quite another to determine its significance and have it drive critical processes.

According to John Rossman, former Amazon executive and author of *The Amazon Way on IoT: 10 Principles for Every Leader from the World's Leading Internet of Things Strategies,* you need to do more than just collect that data; you must relentlessly analyze it. The IoT will help you collect data on your operations at a scale and magnitude beyond anything you've seen before, Rossman says, but the data isn't enough. You need to leverage that data with models, analytics, and algorithms that help you generate insight from it:

> "Your operations can give you much better data, which can tell you what's happening within your organization," Rossman says. "With that, you can strive to create a formulaic understanding of your processes that will give you more insight and definition to tighten up and reinvent those processes."[11]

If your company hasn't already invested in data analytics, make certain that whatever platform you invest in is scalable.

Cisco has predicted that, by 2020, the IoT will create a staggering 6 ZB of data per year![12] However, just because you have huge volumes of data available doesn't mean you must use them all. As Matthew Perry wrote in "Evaluating and Choosing an IoT Platform":

> Data storage is perhaps the most critical tool of all. Buying more storage capacity may seem like an obvious answer, but it's a shortsighted one. Storing bytes of data at orders of magnitude beyond what is actually needed is expensive, and the storage methods can quickly become unwieldy.
>
> Industry experts must evaluate priority data streams and determine who will access them and when.[13]

Harkening back to the issue of Collective Blindness, be particularly aware that the sudden availability of realtime data where you were previously clueless may lead your data analysis into highly specialized areas that you simply couldn't have foreseen. It may require specialized analytical tools and adding trained data scientists to your staff, while also promising insights as a result that may lead to equally unforeseen opportunities.

One striking example of this phenomenon is a Swiss company, AGT. Its "AI Commentator" software (more about combining Artificial Intelligence and the IoT later in this chapter) connects to a variety of sensors placed throughout a sports or entertainment venue including "audio, video, and wearables covering the athletes, coaches, spectators, and remote audience." It interprets this data on the fly and adds an AI component to create unique content designed to increase the audience's involvement.[14] For instance:

At the 2016 New York Fashion Week, it analyzed a broad range of audience and model data, including runway clapping, conversations, outfits, and motions to create hundreds of stories and videos, which resulted in an increase of 4,700 percent in content reach, compared with the previous event.[15]

That seems like a pretty frivolous use of the IoT, but substitute some crucial sector of the economy (AGT also serves industrial IoT and energy clients, for example) and its approach is likely to be a precursor of extremely valuable services that capitalize on realtime data plus AI. How might that apply to your business?

Similar to adding cutting-edge technology such as AI to the Internet of Things is the necessity to choose platforms and other tools that will help you create fluid IoT strategies that can adapt rapidly as other complementary technologies are introduced.

SlantRange is a particularly relevant example. Its founders spent the decade prior to founding the company creating imaging and analytics systems for the military's drone programs. They've adapted that expertise to agriculture, collecting data from another emerging technology—drones—that have special sensors that measure crop health and growth, to help farmers optimize their yields. The approach combines remote sensing and in-field analytics and capitalizes on combining precise data from new high-speed and variable-rate planting equipment, sensors to measure and regulate watering, and monitors at harvest to create previously unobtainable precise data about the entire growth cycle, even in remote growing areas.[16]

And sometimes, it may be very, very simple data collected through the IoT that's all that's needed, such as simplifying logistics with RFID tags that make it possible to identify the exact location of construction equipment. It's simple but critical data that couldn't be gathered before the IoT.[17]

EDGE COMPUTING

Because of the huge volumes of IoT data, engineers realized that it didn't make sense to send all of that data to a central analysis center, especially since much of the data would inevitably be the same (such as data from a smoothly running assembly line). After all, in most cases, what really interests you are the relatively rare deviations from the norm. Edge computing deals with that issue by processing the data at the "edge," near the sensor or other device that collected it. This cuts down on bandwidth needs and makes certain that, where the data may trigger action by a M2M device, there's no latency between collecting the data and acting on it.

PLATFORMS

VHS vs. BetaMax. DVD vs. Blu-Ray. They remind us of the high stakes of picking the wrong platform. That's even more the case with the IoT, because of the Essential Truth about sharing data rather than hoarding it: the sensor you buy may be great, but if the platform it's based on is proprietary or becomes obsolete, you won't be able to realize the full IoT potential of mashing up unlikely data sources in amazing new combinations.

Platforms allow the sharing of IoT data. They are the middleware that takes data from sensors and devices and turns it into valuable results and actions. IoTIFY, a sensor simulation platform company, offers a comprehensive list of criteria for evaluating whether competing IoT platforms are robust and flexible enough:

1. Scalability
2. Bandwidth
3. Protocol (make sure it can support not only current ones such as MQTT and HTTP but also emerging ones)
4. System performance (for example, how long does it take to trigger an action in response to sensor data)
5. Security
6. Redundancy and disaster recovery
7. Hybrid cloud (this might, for example, combine on-site processing for mission critical data and cloud processing for the rest)
8. Solution lifetime (can it, for example, be transferred to another vendor if your current one goes out of business?)
9. Interoperability (perhaps the most important because of the Essential Truth about the need to share data—open source standards are increasingly important to assure this).
10. Edge intelligence

Relatedly, "The future of IoT platform is moving toward distributed, offline, edge intelligence. As devices become more powerful, they can make an autonomous decision based upon local data rather than delegating every decision to cloud. This approach requires that your IoT platform needs to be able to extend itself seamlessly from cloud to fog and even mist and support new topologies for decentralized computing."[18]

As a result, most of the leading internet infrastructure firms, including AT&T, Amazon Web Services, GE (Predix), IBM (Watson), Cisco Jasper, Siemens (MindSphere), Libelium (Waspmote), and my client PTC (ThingWorx) have created robust IoT platforms.

SENSORS

The last IoT components are the ones most specifically identified with it rather than with digitalization in general. They are sensors, the parts that typically cost the least and also get the least-focused attention by management. Sensors are the most critical for creating the IoT, so it's important you have a basic understanding of them. It's at the sensor, whether in a vineyard, in or on your body, on an assembly line, or in a speeding car, where the critical transition is made between analog and digital.

The sensor converts analog signals about changing conditions in the physical world (sound levels, heat, vibration, metal fatigue, moisture, or other variables) are converted into digital signals that are conveyed to the processor, quantified, analyzed, then acted upon.

The possibility of adding sensors to a growing range of products and to a growing range of functions within those products is dramatically increasing as micro-electromechanical systems (MEMS) technology becomes cheaper and smaller. Equally important, new ways of powering them make it easier to use sensors in places where it's hard to replace batteries. For example, researchers at Harvard and the University of Illinois have used 3-D printing to create lithium-ion batteries the size of a grain of sand![19]

Today the number and variety of sensors are increasing exponentially, driven in part by the IoT. Allied Market Research (AMR) predicts that the global market of sensors and actuators (which trigger a M2M response to sensor data so that a machine's operations can be automatically fine-tuned rather than having to wait for human intervention) will average a compound annual growth rate of 11.3 percent until 2022. At that point the market will be $241 billion. The report says the IoT, Industrie 4.0, and wearables will be key drivers.[20]

When the IoT is fully implemented, sensors will become an automatic part of product design, built in at the very beginning of the production process so that they will not only monitor conditions in the field after their sale, but also possibly when they are on the assembly line itself, as part of quality control.

However, for certain manufacturers an ideal way of beginning IoT implementation today with little expense and big potential savings is with Augury's handheld Auguscope. Plant personnel can carry it anywhere in the building where it's needed to analyze how a conventional, no-sensor HVAC system is working. A magnetic sensor temporarily attaches to the machine and the data flows from the Auguscope to the cloud, where it is analyzed to see if the sound is deviating from prerecorded normal sounds, indicating maintenance is needed.

Consistent with other IoT products that are marketed as services instead of sold, Augury uses a "Diagnostics as a Service" model: there are no up-front costs, and customers pay as they go. The company hopes that the technology will eventually be built into household appliances such as washers and dryers.[21]

Using Auguscope is an ideal first step with the IoT because it can be implemented quickly, pays rapid bottom-line benefits, and therefore may lure skeptical senior management who might then be willing to try bolder measures.

Selecting which sensors to use involves key questions involving the IoT product or service's lifecycle operating costs and vulnerability to attack.

- If installed on expensive and durable capital equipment, will they last the full lifespan of the equipment?
- Because they will be built to last, can they also be easily upgraded by new firmware as the nature of security threats changes over time?
- If they are installed in locations that are hard to service, can their energy needs be reduced to a bare minimum, or can the batteries that power them be improved to increase the time between replacements?

One versatile startup, Spain's Libelium, makes the selection process easier by offering a one-stop-shopping site, The IoT Marketplace, that integrates packages from sensors to connectivity and allowing access to any cloud platform. After one year, the site already offers sixty IoT kits, with forty-one partner companies, and provides solutions for nine vertical markets: Cities, Buildings, Agriculture, Environment, Air Quality, Water, Parking, Factory, and eHealth.[22]

Libelium CEO Alicia Asín says that she thinks of the IoT as like a new railway age, and with sensors as the tracks that provide the infrastructure. "Interoperability is the key, which is why we've worked so hard to create partnerships with so many companies."[23]

You might think that if you install one type of sensor on your products or assembly line you'd be set to enjoy full IoT benefits, but not so fast: remember the "share data, not hoard it" Essential Truth. There's growing evidence that IoT benefits multiply when you merge data from a variety of sensors with virtual sensor networks (VSNs). That enables collaborative and efficient wireless sensor networks (WSNs) that combine data from several sensors based on the phenomenon they track or task they perform, such as:

- "Geographically overlapped applications, e.g., monitoring rockslides and animal crossing within a mountainous terrain. Different types of devices that detect these phenomena can relay each other for data transfer without having to deploy separate networks."
- "Logically separating multipurpose sensor networks, e.g., smart neighborhood systems with multifunctional sensor nodes."
- "Enhanc[ing] efficiency of systems that track dynamic phenomena such as subsurface chemical plumes that migrate, split, or merge. Such networks may involve dynamically varying subsets of sensors."[24]

The network concept is enabled by "sensor fusion," which uses a microcontroller to fuse data collected from various sensors to get a more accurate understanding. This leads to potentially amazing applications:

This data, along with the IoT's access to the "global neural network in the sky" and cloud-based processing resources, will lead to a tremendous expansion in the delivery of context-aware services customized for any given situation. Services could be based on the context of what an individual user is doing, what machines are doing, what the infrastructure is doing, what nature is doing, or all of the above in various combinations.[25]

INCORPORATING EMERGING TECHNOLOGIES

One of the IoT's greatest strengths is that it is not a standalone technology, but a variety of technologies that become more valuable when combined. As a result, the IoT will only grow stronger as complementary technologies emerge and mature, including 3-D printing, blockchain, and Artificial Intelligence.

For the near future, 3-D printing will be primarily used for proof-of-concept and prototyping, reducing time-to-market for new products. But consider a day in which the cost and time to print a part are both reduced. Imagine a scenario in which a jet engine's sensors reveal that a part will need to be replaced in the near future. Instead of shipping that replacement from a depot where millions of parts might be stored, the manufacturer might instead send the digital blueprints for the part to a local distribution hub, where a 3-D printer would produce it and the shipping company would deliver it to the airport before the plane lands, reducing the manufacturer's costs for maintaining replacement parts and assuring replacement within minutes. Everyone wins.

Artificial Intelligence has really become viable in the past five years, driven by the exploding volume of data from the IoT and other sources and by increasingly powerful analytical tools such as IBM's Watson to make sense of that data.

An excellent example is iRobot's Roomba vacuums. The new 900 series added a range of AI functions, including "Vision Simultaneous Localization and Mapping," plus better sensors to gather more realtime data. The resulting machine learning has led to new customer services, including Amazon Alexa commands ("Alexa, ask Roomba to begin cleaning") and producing a "clean map" of an entire floor that shows information such as where the Roomba encountered more dirt on the app that controls the Roomba.

The new Roomba illustrates the closed-loop relationship between the IoT's ability to gather data and AI's ability to process it. As perhaps the most comprehensive report on the combination, PWC's *Leveraging the Upcoming Disruptions From AI and the IoT*, emphasized, each provides a vital component for the other: AI makes the vast quantities of data harvested from IoT devices valuable, while the IoT is the best source of the realtime data AI needs to digest to learn and progress:

> Data is only useful if it is actionable. And to make data actionable, it needs to be supplemented with context and creativity. It is about "connected intelligence"—which is where AI and smart machines come into the equation. AI impacts IoT solutions in two key dimensions—firstly in enabling realtime responses, for example via a remote video camera

reading license plates or analyzing faces; and secondly in post-event processing, such as seeking out patterns in data over time and running predictive analytics.

The interdependence between IoT and AI also works the other way. IoT's capacity to enable realtime feedback is critical to adaptive learning systems, since other technologies do not really enable this advanced type of AI/analytics. So they both need each other.[26]

PWC predicts that the combination will lead to truly smart machines: "The ongoing advance of AI is also having a further impact: It's causing AI to converge with IoT, to the extent that it's rapidly becoming indispensable to IoT solutions. The core components of IoT—connectivity, sensor data, and robotics—will ultimately lead to a requirement for almost all 'dumb' devices to become intelligent. In other words, the IoT needs smart machines. Hence the need for AI."[27]

The smart machines will allow unprecedented precision based on M2M communication and self-regulation, which a later chapter will deal with at length.

Blockchain is the technology underlying the bitcoin alternative currency. Ironically, given bitcoin's use in "cryptocrime" schemes, it is now gaining mainstream acceptance, and institutions in the financial, manufacturing, and medical fields, among others, are giving it serious consideration.[28]

Blockchain makes absolutely no sense in the old economy, when protecting data meant writing it in a ledger that you kept in your sweaty little hands or locked in a safe overnight. Instead, complex transactions or data are divided into thirty-two-digit blocks, with each stored on an individual PC anywhere in the world. The key protection is that once the data has been broken up into the blocks, the contents can't be altered without consensus by *all* of the blockholders. This means it:

- **Is transparent.**
- **Can trace all aspects of actions or transactions.** This is critical for complex sequences of actions in an IoT process.
- **Is distributed.** There's a shared form of recordkeeping that everyone in the process can access.
- **Requires permission to change.** Everyone has permission for every step
- **Is secure.** No one person—even a system administrator—can alter it without group approval.

To add a new transaction to the blockchain, all the members must validate it by applying an algorithm to confirm its validity.[29]

The blockchain can also increase efficiency by reducing the need for intermediaries, and it's a much better way to handle the massive flood of data that will be generated by the IoT.

The Chain of Things think tank and consortium is taking the lead on exploring blockchain's application to the IoT. The group describes itself as "technologists at the nexus of IoT hardware manufacturing and alternative blockchain applications." They've run several blockchain hackathons and are working on open standards for IoT blockchains.

Contrast blockchain with the current prevailing IoT security paradigm. As Datafloq points out, it's based on the old client-server approach, which really doesn't work with the IoT's complexity and variety of connections: "Connection between devices will have to exclusively go through the internet, even if they happen to be a few feet apart." It doesn't make sense to try to funnel the massive amounts of data that will result from widespread deployment of billions of IoT devices and sensor through a centralized model when a decentralized, peer-to-peer alternative would be more economical and efficient.

Datafloq concludes:

Blockchain technology is the missing link to settle scalability, privacy, and reliability concerns in the Internet of Things. Blockchain technologies could perhaps be the silver bullet needed by the IoT industry. Blockchain technology can be used in tracking billions of connected devices, enable the processing of transactions and coordination between devices; allow for significant savings to IoT industry manufacturers. This decentralized approach would eliminate single points of failure, creating a more resilient ecosystem for devices to run on. The cryptographic algorithms used by blockchains, would make consumer data more private.[30]

COMPONENTS IN PLACE FOR
IoT BREAKOUT

It took many years for the IoT to get from the early visionaries' dreams to the current early stage of implementation. Now all of the components are in place for a rapid acceleration as awareness of the benefits spreads and the price of components continues to plummet. As we will see in the next chapter, the only remaining obstacle to full realization is our failure to make the mind shifts needed to implement them.

SELF-ASSESSMENT

1. Which of the IoT components does your company already have in place? Given that combination, where does it make sense for you to begin with an IoT strategy?

2. If you don't already have them, big data storage and analysis are probably the IoT tools with the biggest overall payoffs. What are your strategies to get them, and are your solutions scalable to handle the huge increase in data volumes that the IoT will produce?

3. What processes and factors in your products and their production could sensors monitor, and what would the benefits be? If you are already deploying sensors, do you also have plans for IoT platforms that would help merge data from a number of sensor sources?

Digital Twins

A Key IoT Tool—and Dramatic Proof of Its Benefits

E ven though it may not be part of every IoT project today, one IoT tool demands a chapter to itself, because it is both a key tool and perhaps the best and most easily understood—and seen—example of how the IoT merges the digital and physical.

The digital twin is the concept of combining realtime sensor data, analytical tools including Artificial Intelligence, and software to create a realtime wireframe visual model of a physical object and its current status (including its dynamics, if it moves) throughout its lifespan, from the design phase through manufacturing, operations, and finally, disposal. It is continually updated as conditions change and can even incorporate historical data based on past operating conditions.

"The digital twin is meant to be an up-to-date and accurate copy of the physical object's properties and states, including shape, position, gestures, status and motion."[1] Digital twins were impossible until recent technological advances and dramatic price drops in cloud storage, supercomputing, and sensors.

A Siemens video about how Maserati used their digital twin technology to create a sports car made the point visually. First you see a real Maserati barreling toward you at high speed, and then suddenly it morphs into a wireframe computer model of the car: digital and physical merged!

That picture, however, doesn't really do justice to an actual digital twin's visual impact and how helpful it is. To get the most out of this chapter, do yourself a favor: please put down the book, search for "digital twin" on YouTube, watch one or more videos of them in action, and then resume reading!

It is hard to fully appreciate what a crucial role the digital twin can play in helping achieve the Essential Truths discussed previously and realize the IoT's full potential to transform *every* aspect of your strategy and execution.

Think of the digital twin in the context of the Collective Blindness described earlier. The digital twin destroys Collective Blindness about what happens with a product after it leaves the factory and is in daily use. The physical object may be operating on the other side of the world, may be massive, may be impenetrable to the naked eye, but you can sit at your computer and use the digital twin to analyze in realtime every aspect of how that thing is working—or not.

In fact, GE projects that the digital twin concept may eventually be extended to non-manufactured items, such as us: conceivably, every human would have a digital twin from birth. It would grow and change as we do and yield much more nuanced and valuable data about our health, because it would track how the whole body works together, rather than just individual organs in isolation from each other.

Creating a digital twin can be an incremental process, starting with just a few key performance indicators such as temperature, then adding more sensors over time to make it more robust and informative. The more realtime data is fed back from the field to the design studios, assembly line, maintenance department, and even marketing, the more the twin learns and the more valuable it becomes. It will be able to answer questions such as:

- How efficiently is the product running?
- Are certain parts encountering more wear and tear due to their design or operating conditions and are they likely to fail soon?
- If you're trying to maximize efficient operation of a large number of the same product located near each other, how can they each be fine-tuned to work better together?
- Are there functions that internally we thought were important but owners aren't using, and should we either promote them more heavily and provide guidance on how to use them, or eliminate them from future models?
- Were there some potential mistakes in operating the device that we didn't consider during the design phase and which might cause a problem—or danger?
- How is the operator using the product differently from what we visualized, and does that suggest possible enhancements in the next version to incorporate these work-arounds?

- Could the operating data from the field be mashed up with third-party data such as atmospheric conditions, and/or shortages of vital things such as water to create new services that might be valuable to the customer *and* create new revenue streams?

Reflect on those difficult questions. Could you ever imagine that a time might come when we could answer them not just with guesses, but hard, realtime data?

Most important, especially for the concept of the "Circular Company" that will be discussed at length in Chapter 8, no one department or function "owns" the digital twin. The realtime data can be shared by all groups and departments within the company, and on a realtime basis, not sequentially, as in the past.

That's critical.

It means, as IoT entrepreneur Chris Rezendes likes to say, that everyone (and that can include your suppliers, distribution network, retailers, and even customers, if you choose to include them) can share that data, establishing "ground truth" that everyone can operate on, rather than simply guessing or relying on secondhand information as in the past. Or, as analyst Daniel Newman puts it:

It's no secret that silos don't work well in the digital environment. Digital twins help knock those silos down by making data and knowledge available to everyone who needs it—in ways that empower them to keep the system and company moving forward.[2]

Digital twins had their origins in CAD-CAM software used to design products (and even further back, in the analog era, with NASA. It was absolutely critical to know about the condition of a space vehicle, and a little hard to get that information by conventional means!), but those diagrams were usually filed away after the design was completed, because there was no role for them until it was time to design an upgrade.[3]

Until recently, the final step in the design process was usually creation of physical models, because software's ability to actually simulate the device in operation was limited. In 2002, manufacturing expert Dr. Michael Grieves of the University of Michigan first wrote of the digital twin concept because he wanted to extend the digital design model's usefulness throughout the manufacturing process, use, and finally, disposal, as part of product lifecycle management (PLM). As Grieves said, "Stripping information off a physical object is a game changer."[4]

The digital twin will have benefits throughout that product lifecycle:

- **Design.** Not unlike what VisiCalc did for ledgers, it will facilitate exploring design "what ifs," because it will be so easy and inexpensive to play around with product variations during the design process (compared to the time and cost of having to create physical models in the past, and the difficulty or even danger of doing real-life modeling). According to Dr. Grieves, GM now no longer tests its engine designs before production—it simulates their operations.[5] GE's William Ruh says they can now launch products in three to nine months that used to take three years, because of continuous feedback from the products in the field.[6]

- **Manufacturing.** The Siemens Factory of the Future in Amberg also includes a digital twin of the assembly line. "This digital twin is identical in every respect and is used to design the control units, test them, and simulate how to make them and program production machines."[7] Siemens even requires that its suppliers furnish digital twins of their products before the factory begins production of a new item. That way they can see the cascading benefits and increase in precision not only in the assembly line itself, but also integration with suppliers, for a continuous flow and no interruptions.

- **Service.** Technicians won't have to guess what part needs servicing. They will be able to visualize it in advance. In particular, PTC's Vuforia app allows technicians to see inside a device using augmented reality to diagnose the problem— even if they are thousands of miles away and the device is still operating, so that technicians no longer have to randomly tinker when a device is turned off in order to find the problem. Even better, the replacement part can be delivered before they begin the repair, avoiding delays with conventional repairs while a needed part is finally identified and delivered to the repair site.[8]

   In a situation where split-second timing is critical, a twin can alert a pit crew that a key part on a McLaren race car is about to fail, speeding pit stops.[9]

- **Smart Cities.** Singapore will be the first city to have a digital twin. According to *Tech Insider*, "Virtual Singapore incorporates all sorts of data—including climate, demographics, energy consumption, building elevation, and even the location of trees—to create a virtual version of the urban area that can be used to figure out the impact of everything from an influx of wind energy to better disaster management planning. 'You can click on a building and see the surface of its roof, how much electricity it consumes,' Bernard Charlès, CEO of Dassault Systèmes, tells *Tech Insider.* 'You can simulate how in the event of a gas leak or a bombing, the population could escape based on where people are. We have simulation engines for this.'"[10]

- **Healthcare.** Literally getting personal, Dassault (like PTC, another longtime CAD-CAM software designer) has created a "Living Heart" digital twin. It hopes to copy other organs next. This could allow "doctors to replace generic assumptions with individual ones and then digitally probe individuals."[11] Talk about personalized medicine!

With digital twins, you'll begin to think differently about every aspect of products, their design, construction, and use. It's no longer a linear process where you lose track of products once they leave the factory. Consistent with the "close the loop" IoT Essential Truth, these products instead become the hub of your daily routine. An integrated, continuous, cyclical process replaces discrete products. You'll focus on meeting customers' needs in the most efficient way possible—which may mean less emphasis on sales and more on value-added services. In fact, PTC Senior Vice President for Strategy Don Busiek said that he thinks "the digital twin can be the key to the next evolution of our values. We must think of products holistically, from the beginning of design until when we retire it."

Analysts say the impact will be huge: Gartner (which picked "digital twins" as its #4 top strategic technology trend for 2018) predicts half of large industrial companies will use digital twins by 2021, and those companies will gain an average of 10 percent in effectiveness.[12] IDC's prediction is that companies using digital twins will get 30 percent cycle-time improvements with critical processes.[13]

THE BENEFITS REQUIRE WORK

That's not to say that digital twins should be a default part of every IoT product or process, or that the benefits will roll out automatically. Some products may be low-value or disposable and not warrant the time, effort, and expense to create the twins; in other cases, simple monitoring data from the sensors may be adequate feedback.

Gartner Research Vice President Alfonso Velosa, noting twins' ability to monitor and control both assets and processes, has this recommendation for CIOs:

"Work with business leaders to develop economic and business models that consider the benefits in light of the development costs, as well as ongoing digital twin maintenance requirements." The economic value of digital twins will vary widely, depending on the monetization models that drive them. For complex, expensive industrial or business equipment, services, or processes, improving utilization by reducing asset downtime and lowering overall maintenance costs will be extremely valuable, making internal software competencies critical to driving value with digital twins. . . .

"The complexity of digital twins will vary based on the use case, the vertical industry and the business objective. In some cases, we will have simple, functional digital twins that are based on clearly defined functional or technical parameters," Velosa says. "In other cases, they may require physics-based high-fidelity digital twins. In still other cases, there are compound systems composed of other digital twins that need to be integrated."[14]

The process will be continuous because of the tremendous amount of data gathered and its changeability over time. Creating and maintaining the twins will require new software designers and data analysts.

GE DIGITAL WINDFARM

A detailed examination of one of the most advanced and complex digital twin projects will illustrate how transformative they can be.

GE is the company most identified with commercialization of the digital twin concept, having deployed more than 800,000 of them. Its Digital Windfarm suite of advanced turbine hardware and accompanying IoT software (again, the physical-digital merger) includes a crucial digital twin component. The twin is not just for an individual turbine, but for the entire "farm," since the turbines must not only be

THE FUTURE IS SMART

managed individually, but also constantly fine-tuned so that they work optimally as a group (the operation of one turbine affects the operation of those behind it).[15] It's hard to imagine how difficult this task is, because it involves not just costly and complex hardware, but also constantly changing weather conditions that can wreak havoc with the turbines and with the crucial electrical output—or, more positively, if weather conditions are predicted to be optimal, can also be used to boost the efficiency and output. That doesn't even figure in the equally fast-changing and arcane power grid economics and regulation. GE uses the digital twin of the entire farm *before* the turbines are installed, to precisely configure each one for maximum performance by the whole array. The goal is increasing efficiency by 20 percent. "For every physical asset in the world, we have a virtual copy running in the cloud that gets richer with every second of operational data," says Ganesh Bell, Chief Digital Officer and General Manager of Software & Analytics at GE Power & Water.[16]

As Dr. Colin Parris, GE's VP for software, puts it, the digital twin works in three stages: "see, think, and do."[17] First it gathers all sorts of data from the sensors on the turbines, then it analyzes the data and actually runs a wide range of simulations on the GE Predix IoT platform to decide what the range of options is (not just considering the operating data, but also factors such as revenue generation), then it weighs risks and benefits, and finally recommends the best course of action. Ultimately, the digital twin lets you do the right thing at the right time, either providing a human operator with precise instructions or, perhaps, to maximize the precision and accuracy, triggering a specific app that will make the adjustments automatically. Want to go whole hog? You can even don a Microsoft Hololens VR headset, and really "see" what's happening with the turbine, what Parris calls a "much more immersive environment"— even if you're thousands of miles from the windfarm itself. It communicates, as he says, with a "richness of voice and vision that is usually unbelievable."[18]

The system actually improves over time, as more data is collected. This lets it become more predictive and to "future proof" windfarms by maintaining top performance and avoiding the maintenance issues that typically occur as turbines age. It also reduces costs by customizing maintenance schedules to ensure preventive maintenance is done only when needed.

So what benefits do GE's customers get from switching to the Digital Windfarm hardware and software?

One of those customers, Exelon, is working with GE to gain a competitive edge through output both in realtime and a week in advance, which is crucial in the volatile renewable energy market to capture margin price spread and cut forecast-to-actual deviation penalties.[19]

Another customer, E.ON, increased the actual energy produced (AEP) by 469 of its wind turbines by 4 percent in the first year—equal to adding ten costly new turbines.[20]

GE already applies digital twins throughout its product line. One of the most interesting applications is jet engines. Because the engines are used not only under demanding aerial conditions but also on the ground (ones that fly to the Middle East must be serviced more frequently because of the high sand content in the air), the digital twins allow them to pull individual engines for service at different rates depending on their actual usage patterns.[21]

AUGMENTED REALITY PUTS AN END TO
COLLECTIVE BLINDNESS

PTC, which got its start in CAM-CAD and thus has a long history in wireframe representations of things, is also a digital twin leader with a distinct advantage. Several years ago, the company made an investment that made no sense to most: it bought augmented reality pioneer Vuforia.

As *CAD Place* wrote, visionary PTC CEO Jim Heppelmann saw what others didn't: a version of AR-enhanced digital twins in which "the digital model is not only digitally perfect, but where the digital and the real come together, meet, interact, and are—literally—linked together."[22]

PTC's digital twins really drive the final nail in our past Collective Blindness's coffin: users can "see" inside a massive structure using the Vuforia app, as I had an opportunity to do at the company's LiveWorx conference. Suddenly, the Caterpillar power generator appeared to flow apart, and it was possible to visualize the machine's inner workings. Using realtime data from its sensors, I could spot where the repair was needed.[23]

As PTC Executive Vice President Michael Campbell told me, "AR is very compelling because it imposes a very low cognitive load. Otherwise I'd have to sift through all this data myself and it wouldn't be compelling. AR creates insights from data then drives them back into the physical world, just like the digital twin does. Just in terms of the safety implications for workers, how do I understand things that I can't see? AR was the only answer."[24]

PTC has integrated Vuforia Studio with its product lifecycle management program, WindChill, validating real digital twin theorist Michael Grieves's 2002 suggestion that the twin concept could follow a product through its entire lifecycle. Content creators can build intuitive AR experiences for connected products without needing programming expertise.

With the digital twin, we need no longer dream about the IoT's potential to revolutionize every aspect of business: we can see it right before our eyes. As GE's Parris said:

> As we go into the era of the emergence, we have the minds of the humans—maybe 6 billion of them—talking to the minds of the machines, 50 billion of them. That convergence is going to change everything we know.[25]

You bet.

SELF-ASSESSMENT

1. Do you think the digital twin is not only an important IoT tool, but also epitomizes the "smart, connected device" vision?

2. Why would it be valuable for product designers to be able to easily visualize how a product is being used in the field via a digital twin?

3. Why would it be valuable for a product maintenance person to be able to visualize a problem in a product while it is actually in operation (vs. when it is stationary)?

4. As in the case of the GE Digital Windfarm, why would it be valuable to see how a complex of smart, connected devices (vs. a single one in isolation) operates as a whole?

5. How would the advent of widespread use of augmented reality apps and devices supplement the digital twin?

PART II: **LEARNING FROM THE PIONEERS**

5

Siemens and GE

Old War Horses Leading the IoT Revolution

Engineers at Siemens's Munich software center have a dress code requirement their Silicon Valley counterparts don't: Valley folks may kick back and wear sandals, but the Germans must wear steel-toed shoes.

That's because their offices are tucked into a corner of a nineteenth-century locomotive factory that Siemens still operates, manufacturing the company's Vectron locomotives. When the software engineers need a reality test for their innovations, they can just step gingerly and go visit their locomotive design counterparts.

As we turn our focus in this part of *The Future Is Smart* to actually creating and executing an IoT strategy, you need look no further than Siemens and its U.S. counterpart, GE: two of the oldest companies in the world, still manufacturing locomotives *and* creating twenty-first-century software to power the IoT transformation. In large part their street cred comes from the fact that they don't just design IoT software for others, but also use it themselves every day to manufacture, run, and maintain their own products in totally new ways.

For all their own distinctive products and services, there are startling parallels between the two that are relevant to this book, particularly for readers whose companies have been unaware of the IoT or are modestly testing the waters. Both Siemens and GE have fully committed to the IoT and are radically reinventing themselves, their products, and their services.

At the same time, they are not abandoning the physical for the digital: they still make products such as trains and large medical diagnostic devices that remain necessary in the new economy, and those devices (as well as the new software lines) are used by many other companies in their own manufacturing. Both companies aren't just testing the IoT: they are on the bleeding edge of innovation in terms of both IoT technology and services.

Siemens and GE embody most of the marks of the IoT company outlined in the first chapter:

1. Unprecedented assembly line precision and product quality
2. Drastically lower maintenance costs and product failure
3. Increased customer delight and loyalty
4. Improved decision making
5. Ability to create new business models and revenue streams

And, while they haven't formally addressed the sixth IoT hallmark, the circular management organization, both companies exhibit management characteristics consistent with it.

Bottom line: *if these two relics of the early Industrial Age can make the IoT transformation, why can't you?*

SIEMENS

Siemens is 170 years old. It began with Werner Siemens's pointer telegraph and really attained prominence in 1866 with the dynamo, which began the electrical engineering era by converting mechanical energy to electricity. Its other early firsts included the first electrical railway in 1879 and the first subway in continental Europe in 1896. The company was an early medical innovator, creating the first industrially manufactured X-ray tubes for medical diagnostics in 1896. In 1953, Siemens was first to use ultrasound for echocardiography. In 1983, Siemens introduced the MRI scanner.

However, the Siemens innovation that perhaps was the most important precursor of its eventual emergence as an IoT powerhouse was the Simatic transistorized control and instrumentation system introduced in 1958, replacing conventional relays, contractors, and electron tubes and "making it possible to build circuits for logical connections, storage, counting, and computing."[1] Various Simatic control systems are used at most manufacturing plants, and the devices have constantly evolved with progress in communications technology.

The company's innovations in industrial automation are now associated with the concept of the digital factory. "Siemens set the course for the digital automation of entire production facilities as far back as 1996, when the launch of its Totally Integrated Automation (TIA) Portal enabled companies to coordinate elements of their production operations and to closely intermesh hardware with software."[2]

Siemens has benefited in recent years from the German government's formal strategy for what it calls "Industrie 4.0," to merge physical products with digital controls and communications.[3] The term itself was first used at the Hanover Fair in 2011 and has since become a widespread strategic goal not just in Germany, but Europe as a whole. The initiative is supported by funding from the German Federal Ministry of Education and Research and the German Federal Ministry of Economic Affairs and Energy and emphasizes the merger of the digital and physical in manufacturing through cyber-physical control systems. Because the U.S. federal government doesn't weigh in on specific economic plans to the same extent, the concept is more advanced in Europe, and the term has gathered cachet, especially as specific examples have proved profitable.[4]

The shining example of Industrie 4.0 is the previously mentioned Siemens plant in Amberg. It has increasingly computerized over the past twenty-five years, and now is a laboratory for fusion of the physical and digital.

The plant's 99.99885 percent quality rate would be astounding by any measure but is even more incredible when you realize that it does not do daily repetitions of the same mass-production product run. Instead, Amberg is where the company makes the Simatic programmable logic controls (PLCs) mentioned above that are the heart of its industrial output and which are used worldwide to allow machine-to-machine (M2M) automated assembly line self-regulation. They are made in more than a thousand variations for 60,000 customers worldwide, requiring frequent readjustments of the production line. In one of the ultimate examples of eating your own dog food, a thousand Simatic units are used to control the assembly line. Total output at the factory is 12 million yearly, or approximately one per second.[5]

One downside of the Amberg system's efficiency is that automation has nearly eliminated assembly line jobs: the only time humans touch one of the products is to put the initial circuit board on the assembly line. The 1,100-person workforce deals almost entirely with computer issues and overall supervision of the assembly line. Nevertheless, Siemens doesn't visualize a totally automated, workerless factory in the future:

> "We're not planning to create a workerless factory," says [Plant Manager Professor Karl-Heinz] Büttner. After all, the machines themselves might be efficient, but they don't come up with ideas for improving the system. Büttner adds that the employees' suggested improvements account for 40 percent of annual productivity increases. The remaining 60 percent is a result of infrastructure investments, such as the purchase of new assembly lines and the innovative improvement of logistics equipment. The basic idea here, says Büttner, is that "employees are much better than management at determining what works or doesn't work in daily operation and how processes can be optimized." In 2013 the [plant] adopted 13,000 of these ideas and rewarded employees with payments totaling around €1 million.[6]

As Siemens develops new IIoT software, it is deployed at the Amberg factory to control the Simatic control units, which generate more than 50 million data points daily for analysis. Among other programs, the factory runs the NX and Teamcenter project lifecycle management software, allowing the staff to share realtime insights on the assembly line and fine-tune its operation.

Siemens's strategy of merging the physical and digital has meant that its software offerings constantly expand, and they facilitate the kind of real and virtual collaborative workstyles that will be discussed at length in Chapter 8. Among others, they include offerings that specifically address key aspects of the IoT:

- **Product Lifecycle Management (PLM)** software programs, which let engineers both model new products and extensively test them virtually, without having to build and test physical models. This both cuts costs and allows more experimentation with "what if" variations on a design, because the risk of creating alternatives is so low. As we will see later, products designed with PLM can reach the market 50 percent faster. One particularly interesting part of the PLM offerings is one specifically for additive manufacturing (i.e., 3-D printing), to capitalize on this emerging option. Siemens has brought all of these programs together under the Teamcenter label, emphasizing that it provides an "open framework for interoperability," a critical example of the "share the data" Essential Truth discussed in Chapter 2, allowing anyone who needs it companywide to access critical realtime data.

- **Digital twins,** used in coordination with PLM, discussed earlier as the highest manifestation of the digital/physical synthesis, allow rigorous testing of products before they are launched. Siemens did this with simulations of the NASA Rover Curiosity to prepare for its nail-biting "seven minutes of terror" landing. As one member of the design team said: "We don't get a chance to retry or rebuild or service or redesign. We have one shot—and it's usually doing something we've never done before. We're trying to use existing tools and processes to get us through a unique design."[7]

Perhaps the most important of these software offerings for full realization of the Industrie 4.0 vision is the new combination of Siemens XHQ Operations Intelligence Software with the open-systems Siemens MindSphere cloud that adds advanced analytics and machine learning. Also, because it is cloud-based, the XHQ data can be ported to other cloud-based applications. If your company is considering an IoT initiative, the cloud-based alternative not only can save money compared to self-storage, but also opens the opportunity for using cloud-based Software as a Service (SaaS).

However, most companies, especially those with long records of manufacturing non-IoT devices, will be most interested in what Siemens is doing to make itself a guinea pig and apply its new technologies to its own existing products. How is the IoT helping them to cut their own costs and increase performance and customer satisfaction?

Fittingly, some of the most dramatic examples of Siemens's IoT thinking in action have centered on one of its oldest lines of business: those electric trains invented in the nineteenth century. The company's Railigent IoT system (which connects to its IoT Mindsphere platform) can:

- cut rail systems' operating costs by up to 10 percent
- deliver eye-popping on-time performance (only 1 of 2,300 trains was late!)
- assure 99 percent availability through predictive maintenance

Its new Mobility Services have taken over maintenance for more than fifty rail and transit programs.

Again, the company's years of experience building and operating trains pays off in the cyberworld. Dr. Sebastian Schoning, CEO of Siemens's client Gehring Technologies, which manufactures precision honing tools, told me that it was easier to sell Siemens's digital services to his own client base because so many of the products they already own include Siemens devices, giving his customers confidence in the new offerings.[8]

The key to Siemens's Mobility Services is Sinalytics, its platform architecture for data analysis not just for rail, but also for industries ranging from medical equipment to windfarms. More than 300,000 devices currently feed realtime data to the platform. Sinalytics capitalizes on the data for multiple uses, including connectivity, data integration, analytics, and the all-important cyber security. They call the result not Big Data, but Smart Data. The platform also allows merging the data with data from sources such as weather forecasts, which, in combination, can let clients optimize operating efficiency on a realtime M2M basis.

Elements of an IoT system on the trains that can be adapted to other physical products include:

Sensing. There are sensors on the engines and gearboxes. Vibration sensors on microphones measure noises from bearings in commuter trains. They can even measure how engine oil is aging, so it can be changed when really needed, rather than on an arbitrary schedule, a key predictive maintenance advantage.

- **Algorithms.** These make sense of the data and act on it. They read out patterns, record deviations, and compare them with train control systems or with vehicles of the same type.

- **Predictive maintenance.** This replaces scheduled maintenance, dramatically reducing downtime and catastrophic failure. For example: "There's a warning in one of the windows (of the control center display): engine temperature unusual. 'We need to analyze the situation in greater depth to know what to do next—we call it root cause analysis,' (says) Vice-President for Customer Support Herbert Padinger. 'We look at its history and draw on comparative data from the fleet as a whole.' Clicking on the message opens a chart showing changes in temperature during the past three months. The increased heat is gradually traced to a signal assembly. The Siemens experts talk with the customer to establish how urgent the need for action is, and then take the most appropriate steps."[9] Padinger says that temperature and vibration analyses from the critical gearboxes gives Siemens at least three days advance notice of a breakdown—plenty of time for maintenance or replacement. Predictive maintenance is now the norm for 70 to 80 percent of Siemens's repairs.[10]

- **Security.** This is especially important given all of the miles of track and large crowds on station platforms. It includes video-based train dispatch and platform surveillance using Siemens's SITRAIL D system, as well as cameras in the trains. The protections have to run the gamut from physical attacks to cyber-attacks. For security, the data is shared by digital radio, not networks that are also shared by consumers.[11]

3-D Printed Parts

When operations of physical objects are digitized, it allows seamlessly integrating emerging digital technologies into the services—making these huge engines showcases for the newest technologies. For example, Siemens Digital Services also included augmented reality (so repair personnel can see manuals on heads-up displays), social collaboration platforms, and—perhaps most important—3-D printing-based additive manufacturing, so that replacement parts can be delivered with unprecedented speed. 3-D printing also allows a dramatic reduction in parts inventories. It allows for replacement of parts that may no longer be available through conventional parts depots. It may even improve on the original part's function and durability, based on practical experience gained from observing the parts in use. For example, it's often possible with 3-D printed replacement parts to consolidate three or four separate components into a single one, strengthening and simplifying it. Siemens has used 3-D printing for the past three years, which lets them assure customers that they will have replacement parts for the locomotive's entire lifespan, which can exceed thirty years.

The new Mobility Services approach's results are dramatic:

- None of the Velaro trains that Siemens maintains for several operators have broken down since implementing Sinalytics. Among those in Spain, only one has left more than fifteen minutes behind time in 2,300 trips: a 0.0004 percent lateness rate.
- Reliability for London's West Coast Mainline is 99.7 percent.
- Perhaps most impressive because of the extreme cold conditions it must endure, the reliability rate for the Velaro service in Russia is 99.9 percent.[12]

Siemens's ultimate goal is higher: what the company calls (pardon the pun) 100 percent Railability.

When it does reach those previously inconceivable quality benchmarks, Siemens predicts that, as the software and sensors evolve, the next stage will be new business models in which billing will be determined by guaranteeing customers availability and performance. As we will see in the second half of this chapter, GE (and others) are already doing that with jet turbines, leasing rather than selling them, with the price paid based on the amount of thrust the engines generate, giving GE an extra incentive for predictive maintenance. If the engine is sitting on the ground rather than flying, it isn't bringing in any revenue. Will that someday be the case with railroad engines as well?

Finally, let's look at how Siemens software is being used by other companies to design all-new products: in this case, a sleek, 165 mph Maserati Ghibli. The Siemens brochure accompanying the Maserati case study has a stark warning to manufacturers of all sorts:

> The manufacturing industry is now at the stage where the automation of complete workflows is the only way to ensure a long-term, defendable, competitive position. . . .
>
> Business is becoming more and more impacted by digitalization. Customers are increasingly able to tell manufacturers directly—via the Internet—exactly what they want and when. If manufacturers don't respond, alternatives can often be found easily, and potential business can be lost quickly. . . .
>
> To address this challenge, manufacturers need to significantly reduce their time-to-market, while massively increasing flexibility to enable individualized mass production—and do so with reduced energy and resource consumption. Solutions to address this challenge are developed by initiatives such as the Internet of Things and Industrie 4.0. . . .
>
> The manufacturing industry is now at the stage where the automation of complete workflows is the only way to ensure a long-term, defendable, competitive position.
>
> The experience acquired along the entire value chain then flows back into the design and development processes, creating a beneficial cycle.[13]

Siemens emphasizes that it's not enough to simply digitize the design process. Everything from design through supply chain, manufacturing, distribution, and service must be linked in a continuous digital web, where "complete digital representation of the entire physical value chain is the ultimate goal."

Siemens crafts this circular digitalization through yet another software suite, what it labels the Digital Enterprise Software Suite, including many of the same programs we've already seen that the company depends on for its own manufacturing. It allows the kind of complete modeling of the entire business process mentioned above, including "seamlessly integrating suppliers into the mix." That's a key step toward the vision of the completely circular enterprise that will be discussed at length in Chapter 8.

In the case of designing the new Maserati (as it made the transition from hand-built cars), the carmaker used the NX CAD software for the design, so they could virtually create, simulate, and even test the cars, which both sped the process and reduced the need for costly prototypes. As Maserati's Luca Soriato said, the software let them do "analyses which until recently could only be carried out physically, through the creation of prototypes."[14] The existing plant was almost completely rebuilt to incorporate digitalization.[15]

Equally important, Maserati combined NX with Teamcenter, allowing them to manage the project in realtime despite being located in several areas. That's a great example of the "share data" Essential Truth: if the various parts of the design team worked in isolation from each other, they would not only take more time, with one group handing it off to another (and then having to get back to the original group for any changes based on later contributions), but the chance for error would be greatly increased.

Design time was cut by 30 percent, and time to market was only sixteen months, compared to a three-year industry average. Nor was the human element ignored in all this digitalization.

A development report by business analyst Andrew Hughes points out:

> Since going live Maserati has continued to improve the assembly process, in particular by continuous improvement through assembly workers' suggestions. To date each worker has averaged fifteen suggestions for small process improvements per year, and the vast majority are implemented.[16]

GE

Granted, GE is a mere startup compared to Siemens, since Edison only got around to creating it in 1892 to commercialize his many inventions. Yet it has labored mightily to overcome that upstart status, and in fact entered many of the same industries as Siemens, such as electrical motors, medical diagnostics, and locomotives.

Unfortunately, the company lost some of its focus during the 1990s and first decade of this century and became an ungainly conglomerate, entering the entertainment and financial industries, among others. In the midst of slumping profits during the last decade, CEO Jeff Immelt came to much the same conclusion as Siemens: digitize or die. He divested some of the major investments that diverted GE's focus from manufacturing (as he put it, "I believed that the company couldn't simultaneously be good at media, pet insurance, and making jet engines") and firmly committed GE to what it calls the "Industrial Internet of Things" (IIoT), focusing on manufacturing and heavy industry, while also making a major commitment to globalization.[17]

No Dabbling

If you're cautious and think your IoT strategy might be to put a toe in the water to see if it might work, don't come to Immelt for comfort. As he wrote when he left the company in mid-2017 under pressure from dissatisfied investors, the times require a complete commitment to the change:

> You can't regard a transformation as an experiment. We've approached digital very differently from the way other industrial and consumer products companies have. Most say, "We'll take an equity stake in a digital startup, and that is our strategy." To my mind, that's dabbling. I wanted to get enough scale fast enough to make it meaningful. My view was that GE had as good a chance as anybody at winning in the industrial internet, because we were not starting from scratch: We had a $240 billion installed base of service contracts, a huge order backlog, and the ability to offer financing. We could build on our existing strengths to get even better.
>
> So we launched digital across all our businesses. By that I mean we launched a major effort to embed sensors in our products and build an analytics capability to help our customers learn from the data that the sensors generated. Initially we focused on increasing the productivity of their service contracts—for example, improving the uptime, or the time on wing, of our jet engines and reducing the turnaround time for overhauls. After that we built new capabilities in our businesses and started selling them to our existing customers—helping them use analytics the way we did. Then

we built the Predix platform, which we aimed to make the operating system for the industrial internet.[18]

GE did look at a number of existing IoT platforms but decided none were really adequate for the massive demands of industrial digitalization, so it built the cloud-based Predix, which continues to evolve based on the constant closed-loop flow of data from the factory floor and products in the field. Predix is both the platform for GE's own internal digitization, and, increasingly, is marketing as a cloud-based service platform for others. In 2016, it extended Predix to "edge computing," with the Predix Edge System. That made Predix a distributed operating system rather than just a cloud-based one, so it could analyze data at or close to the sensor where it was collected, because near-instantaneous adjustment of equipment based on the data can be critical to optimizing efficiency and reducing problems. As IDG reported, "The code that shuts down a pipeline in case of a leak should run as close as possible to the leak sensor rather than up in the cloud, where there will be a longer delay before the shutdown command can reach the site."[19]

Immelt set goals for the IIoT transformation that might seem pedestrian, but in fact could have a tremendous impact on the global economy's costs and sustainability if successful—because of its focus on manufacturing things, not sexy social media apps, and because it concentrated on what in fact would be a major shift in the economy, reducing things' operating inefficiency. The specific goal was the "Power of 1%," i.e., making industry worldwide at least 1 percent more efficient by a combination of factors such as reducing downtime and energy consumption, which would result in hundreds of billions of dollars of economic gains. In practice, the results have been far more dramatic, with efficiency increases of 20 percent or more across the industries it focuses on. "These performance gains improve competitiveness and profitability for companies across sectors. And they will deliver a substantial economic gain in terms of stronger growth in jobs and incomes."[20]

Brilliant Factories

Similar to Siemens, much of GE's success since making the IoT commitment has come by a seamless integration between its internal operations and the products and services it offers for sale. In other words, GE has used itself as its laboratory, and IDG cites its internal success as a key marketing strength: "The IDC MarketScape recognized GE's own digital industrial transformation story, citing it as a proof point and appeal for companies that are also embarking on their own digital transformation."[21]

No component of GE's IIoT strategy has emphasized those basics as much as its "Brilliant Factories" initiative. Internally, approximately a hundred of the company's more than five hundred global factories are now classified as brilliant. These facilities combine lean and advanced manufacturing, 3-D printing, and advanced digitalization to maximize productivity and profit. Based on the original success, it is now marketing the services to other companies.

Brilliant Factories are made possible by what the company labels "Brilliant Manufacturing" software, which links every aspect of manufacturing into a seamless whole. The resulting data flows from the sensors in every part of the process and is then analyzed to improve both the products and the processes themselves. The benefits are impressive and touch on every aspect of operations because of the synergies between the individual aspects:

- 10 to 20 percent reduction in unplanned downtime due to better maintenance management through real-time sensor data at GE Transportation's Grove City, Pennsylvania, factory.
- 20 percent inventory reduction at a global consumer packaged goods client.
- 20 percent capacity recovery for a key product category at a global chemical company let it delay spending for a new production line.[22]

Similar to Siemens, GE is even using additive manufacturing through state-of-the-art 3-D printing as part of the Brilliant Factories combination, an exciting example of the IoT's ability (as with augmented reality) to add newly developed digital technologies to the overall mix.

Learn from the Consumer Web

Something GE did in its commitment to the Industrial Internet of Things that other companies should consider was to look closely at the consumer internet and its implications for digitizing. A key part of GE's road map to transformation was achieved in part by locating a major software development facility in San Ramon, hiring Cisco veteran Bill Ruh to run it, and forming collaborations with a number of internet giants. GE also looked carefully at lessons from the success of consumer-focused internet companies. According to GE VP of Software Research Dr. Colin Parris:

> Internet giants like Apple, Google, and Amazon have generated value from the insights of people. People building apps; people searching for items or topics of interest; and people shopping online for things they want to buy. They took all this knowledge shared by human beings and created digital twins of us to construct new business platforms. Apple created the App Store; Google turned "Search" into an "Ad" business; and Amazon built an online retail empire.[23]

As we saw in Chapter 3, one specific crossover from the consumer world is what GE calls "industrial apps," ones specifically designed for remote operation of devices. As former GE Chief Economist Marco Annunziata wrote:

> Industrial apps will bring greater efficiency throughout the economy. They will allow us to produce more energy from renewable sources and use it more efficiently—spurring major changes in the energy industry. They will make healthcare better and more affordable. They will reduce delays in hospitals and airports. Combined with new production techniques, they will help develop manufacturing activities in new places, creating jobs and accelerating growth in emerging economies. Their impact on our lives will be stronger than that of consumer apps—even if it might not be as evident.[24]

Another key element of GE's totally integrated IIoT approach is the switch to predictive maintenance, both internally and as a service to other manufacturers, creating a whole new revenue stream from reducing unplanned maintenance. Predictive maintenance is part of another emerging strategy to consider as part of an overall IoT strategy: asset performance management (APM), which is designed to optimize a company's operational assets such as plants, equipment, and infrastructure by reducing maintenance costs and emergency repairs, and maximizing the assets' availability and overall plant operations efficiency.

It can even lead to totally new marketing strategies, as mentioned previously, where products such as jet turbines are no longer sold, but (because of radically increased dependability and lower repair costs) are leased, with the customer's costs determined by thrust generated or some other new metric. This never would have been possible in the era of Collective Blindness, when manufacturers were clueless about the status of their products once they left the factory.

IIoT Lets GE Go Global

GE's focus has become global, both literally and figuratively. One of Immelt's key priorities was to dramatically increase the company's global revenues from outside the U.S. In 2011, he formed GE's Global Growth Organization, responsible for dramatically expanding its presence in emerging markets. Since then, outside-the-U.S. revenues have grown to $67 billion, or 59 percent of their worldwide total.[25]

By thinking globally in the figurative sense (and fully capitalizing on the "share data, don't hoard it" Essential Truth) the company also realized that IoT lessons from one industry could be applied to others as well. Annunziata has written of the potential to "leverage the power of the 'Global Brain'—the distributed and connected intelligence of millions of people around the globe," for industrial efficiency, just as consumer apps development has become global.[26] Similarly, GE decided to share the results of its IoT initiatives across the company, by creating the GE Store, a horizontal global knowledge exchange that lets all parts of the company leverage one division's data and experiences to create similar innovations in their own sector.

It is hard to quantify, but this aspect of giving free access to data has an additional benefit. Those in another division, with another set of expertise and experiences, may see an entirely different lesson in the same data.

IIoT Has Brought Change, but Results Lag

GE has been universally acknowledged as a leader in the transition to the IIoT, but that doesn't mean it has been easy. Nor have the bottom-line improvements satisfied investors. Immelt left his job earlier than planned in mid-2017, with Wall Street still critical of his management and lackluster results.[27] However, his successor, John Flannery, remains committed to The Industrial Internet of Things:

> We have fully embraced the digital industrial transformation, and we believe in its potential to change the world. For our customers, digital is bringing new levels of innovation and productivity—and they are seeing real, tangible outcomes.

This is happening in each of our businesses. Now, we are taking these outcomes and transferring what we have learned directly to our customers.[28]

Both Siemens and GE are more than a hundred years old, yet they are among the leading Internet of Things companies, in large part because they saw early on that the digital-physical fusion was inevitable and committed fully to making the change. In large part the credibility of their digital offerings comes from the fact that both have used their own internal operations as the laboratories for their new services, exemplifying the digital twins. While your company may not have their deep roots in the Industrial Age, there is much to learn from them about making the IoT leap.

SELF-ASSESSMENT

1. Siemens's software engineers can get an instant reality check simply by walking to the other side of their building to talk with locomotive designers. What can you do to stimulate that same kind of interplay?

2. GE looked to lessons from consumer web giants for types of services they could offer to their industrial customers. Have you ever done a formal analysis of similar lessons from the consumer web for your company? What lessons have you drawn?

3. Both Siemens and GE have used their own operations as the guinea pigs for IoT services they eventually commercialized and marketed for other companies. How could you do that?

4. Both Siemens and GE made full commitments to the Internet of Things early on, rather than just experimenting, because they saw the digital-physical revolution was inescapable for material products. Have you made a similar decision? If not, why not?

6

Smart Companies Already Know
the IoT Is a Game Changer

You may find it hard to identify with Siemens or GE if your company isn't more than a hundred years old and isn't firmly established both in major industrial products *and* IoT software. Fair enough, but the good news is that mainstream companies and government agencies both big and small, old and startup, in every sector of the global economy are already making commitments to the IoT and realizing tangible economic benefits. You are bound to find at least one example among the following that will provide you with a starting point for beginning the conversion to IoT-based strategies.

It's crucial to remember that incremental strategies are viable, especially in what is perhaps the most effective entry point to the IoT: converting your existing equipment to smart devices. Yes, machinery and personal devices designed from the ground up as smart devices are the most cost-effective and efficient but adding sensors gradually over time can in many cases increase efficiency at the beginning and result in astonishing levels of precision and self-regulation.

ACHIEVING UNPRECEDENTED PRECISION AND EFFICIENCY

Perhaps the single most pervasive benefit companies are achieving with the IoT would be sufficient to merit all the attention: unprecedented precision and efficiency. That is logical and predictable if we go back to the reality companies all faced before the Collective Blindness barrier was lifted: there were so many data gaps in the past that it was basically impossible for companies to really coordinate not only between departments within the company, but also with outside partners such as supply chain or distribution networks and retailers, which led to understandable problems such as excessive inventories and/ or parts shortages. (Remember "just-in-time"? It would have been more appropriate to call it "sorta just-in-time.")

Replace those information gaps with shared access to real-time data about production, sales, and repairs, and you can see how realtime collaboration between these players is now possible. With it comes unprecedented precision.

That's equally true within the assembly line itself, especially with M2M controls, where processes can now be minutely adjusted without human intervention.

No wonder smart companies of all sorts and sizes are investing in the IoT.

The ideal first step, because it both minimizes up-front costs and pays short-term benefits in terms of operating efficiency, is to add on sensors to existing manufacturing equipment to allow realtime monitoring of operating conditions. While sensors are now being built into a growing number of assembly-line devices, companies that have large amounts invested in conventional machinery with long lifespans will be most interested in updating their current equipment.

Swedish manufacturer ABB makes this possible with its ABB Ability Smart Sensor, which is attached to one of the most common and oldest types of motors, low-voltage (LV) induction ones. Most of them currently run until they fail due to lack of any advance notice of possible problems. The add-on sensors identify maintenance problems in time for predictive maintenance, as well as avoiding the secondary damage that results when these motors fail, reducing repair and downtime costs. This addresses the causes of about 75 percent of LV motor failures and reduces downtime by about 70 percent.

Perhaps most importantly, the Smart Sensors don't require wiring, further simplifying and reducing the cost of retrofitting. The sensor uses smartphones to send information about the motor's operations to a secure server. Estimated payback time is less than one year.[1]

LOGISTICS AND SUPPLY CHAIN

Anyone who lives in areas of the Northeast where oil heat is the norm can tell you how they'd prefer fewer of the huge delivery trucks trying to navigate residential driveways. (Especially when a truck slides sideways and requires several hours of towing after sliding into your pristine pond. As you may guess, this is not a hypothetical scenario to your author.) The oil delivery business has traditionally been low-tech, and owners have resorted to frequent deliveries when it often turns out oil deliveries weren't needed, rather than deal with angry customers who run out of oil on a bone-chilling winter night.

The IoT has changed all that, while saving the dealers significantly on unneeded deliveries. Senet, a New Hampshire–based Network as a Service (NaaS) M2M operator, is installing 20,000 LoRa sensors paired with IBM software at homes and businesses that track fuel levels in propane and oil tanks. Every hour the sensors collect and securely transmit data, including fuel levels, gauge status, sensor status, and sensor recalibration reports, to fuel providers. LoRa sensors are essential, because they require minimal battery power.

One dealer, James Proulx of Proulx Oil and Propane in New Hampshire, says his company has cut nearly three unneeded trips per customer yearly, delivering more oil each time they do go and cutting their delivery costs because of this realtime data. According to Proulx, because of the IoT "share data" Essential Truth, there's an unexpected customer satisfaction bonus: his customers can also access the data, so they can tell how much oil they have left when they're away from home, rather than having to go to the basement and try to read a primitive float gauge on the tank: "We can remotely see what's in each tank at all times. . . . We now have a better collaborative working relationship with our customers," Proulx says.[2]

As mentioned previously, a good strategy in looking for breakthrough solutions is to look to an organization that faces not just difficult problems but extreme—perhaps even life-or-death—ones, since they're more likely to really think outside the box in search of a solution.

You may think your supply chain is difficult, but does it involve delivering donor organs for transplants not only in time to save someone's life, but in proper condition (i.e., not opened in transit or otherwise compromised)?

That's why hospitals have come to rely on FedEx's innovative SenseAware system. Packages using the premium service, whether a heart or a priceless artifact, are given a smart tag that can detect a range of conditions, such as temperature change or exposure to light (indicating the package was opened). Equally important, the shipper and recipient can access this information in realtime, which can be critical to a hospital in terms of knowing when to prep the recipient and assemble the operating team.

One case highlighted the critical nature of realtime location-based information that SenseAware packages transmit: A kidney was scheduled to be shipped cross country for a transplant but the container missed the plane. Locating it instantly, the shipper determined that it would not be possible to ship it until the next morning, when the kidney would no longer be viable. Instead, again using realtime data, a secondary recipient was located and the kidney successfully delivered to the other hospital in time.[3]

BETTER DECISION MAKING

Companies are finding that the benefits of factorywide monitoring and data analytics for the reams of data they yield include not just smoother operations but also improved decision making. Management has access to realtime data not only from the assembly line but also from the supply chain and other vital information sources that simply weren't available in the past.

Dieter Haban, the CIO at Daimler Trucks North America in Portland, Oregon, which manufactures a wide array of heavy trucks such as Freightliner and Thomas Built, says, "We produce and collect a massive amount of data to understand where we are during the assembly of the truck. Now we can provide dashboard information to management, stay informed about any parts shortages, and know the status of the vehicle in realtime, any time."[4]

Similarly, Mitsubishi and Intel teamed up for another in-plant system, combining sensors plantwide at Intel's Malaysia factory and big data analytics to cut costs by $9 million and improve decision making. The key, Intel reports, is learning to be more creative in handling the big data yielded by monitoring the assembly line: "The real opportunity is how to combine . . . data differently, which will ultimately give you insights not only into how your factory is running but, what's more important, will let you predict how your factory will run the next minute, the next hour, the next shift, the next day." Other benefits include better equipment uptime and predictive maintenance.[5]

Sometimes, simply knowing where things are through geo-location is terribly important. That's the situation in the Port of Hamburg, one of the busiest in the world, and the largest in Germany.[6] One hundred forty million tons of cargo move through it yearly, up to 40,000 trucks arrive daily, and the port directly and indirectly provides 156,000 jobs. The biggest challenge is smooth operation of both the docks and the rails that serve the port, which can't be expanded.

Its management strategy was to create a number of "smart-PORTS" to allow smooth flow of containers through a combination of cloud and realtime traffic management. Its smartPORT logistics platform runs on SAP's Networked Logistics Hub, which in turn draws on data from the SAP HANA Cloud Platform. The result is consolidated data about every container, ship, and truck in the port, which is shared in realtime, resulting in streamlined cargo handling. The system is so granular that not only do trucks get realtime advice on the best route to take, but also, when a truck will be held up at an open drawbridge, the driver gets a discount coupon on his handheld for coffee at a place within walking distance![7]

NEW BUSINESS MODELS/
NEW REVENUE STREAMS

The last of the four IoT Essential Truths was "rethink products and their roles."

This aspect of the IoT is still in its early stages, in large part because it requires that the earlier steps of gaining accurate, realtime data about products' use and their status be fully implemented. When that's done, companies will for the first time have the option of marketing their products differently because they will have true, complete lifecycle costs that they could never access before, and can assure reliability both through improved design and the ability to do predictive maintenance.

One company that has totally rethought its sales model due to the IoT is Winterhalter, Germany's leading manufacturer of commercial dishwashers, which is now offering customers a "pay per wash" option. Their marketing copy says it all: "PAY PER WASH. No Investment. Zero Risk. Winterhalter boosts commercial washing to the next level: the first . . . washer you only pay for when you actually use it. That means perfect wash results for everyone—regardless of the available budget, and with maximum flexibility."

It's a new concept, "servitization": from product selling to the all-inclusive washing service offering. The Winterhalter customer accesses the payment system online, chooses how many wash cycles s/he wants, and pays with a credit card. Just like the systems GE is offering with their jet turbines, the customer only pays for use, not when the washing machine is just sitting there. It's a win-win for all parties:

- The manufacturer gets a predictable revenue flow, rather than onetime sales, increased customer loyalty because of a continuing relationship, and less chance of losing a customer (because a customer whose needs continue to be met is less likely to shop around).
- The customer gets increased dependability based on predictive maintenance, doesn't have to make a major up-front capital investment, may receive improved performance over time through innovations such as software (not just hardware) upgrades, pays only when they actually use the product, and has predictable costs with fewer costly surprises.
- The planet may have fewer products being landfilled because they are upgraded rather than disposed of, and reduced global warming because the products will be run more efficiently.[8]

John Deere is doing the same thing in the oldest industry of all, agriculture. Agriculture is perhaps the most at-risk from global warming, especially due to increasingly wild climate fluctuations that make it difficult to objectively monitor what is happening and, particularly with dwindling water supplies, to know precisely when to irrigate and exactly how much is needed.

John Deere controls an estimated 60 percent of the U.S. farming-equipment market but has suffered from falling revenues in recent years because of declining farm equipment sales. Now it is filling the gap by selling farmers valuable realtime data, mashing up data from its equipment on the farm with Weather Service and other data, to make certain water and fertilizer are applied properly: "A farmer might not have to buy a new piece of equipment every year, but he's still doing the data every year. That part of the business can be more constant," according to CEO Samuel Allen. For example, Deere's SeedStar Mobile app lets farmers monitor spacing between planted seeds and "singulation" (the term that describes the deployment of a seed from the meter, the machine that regulates seed flow) row by row.

More than 200,000 Deere machines can wirelessly transmit agronomic data to remote servers to be organized, analyzed, and mashed up to be used with other applications including coordinating multiple machines in the same field.[9]

SMALL AND MEDIUM BUSINESSES ALSO PROFIT FROM THE IoT

These benefits are all well and good for major companies, but small and medium-sized businesses can be excused for being dubious about whether the IoT's benefits outweigh the costs, especially in its early stages. Wouldn't a prudent IoT strategy for them be to observe the field and wait five years or so until it is more mature and the costs are lower? Several examples show that IoT tools are mature enough, the price has dropped, and—perhaps most important—the price of inaction and the previously unobtainable benefits are so great that action now is prudent.

One important example from agriculture is in vineyards. It's not just irrigation in question but also, for example, monitoring ambient humidity and CO_2 levels that effect the tanins and anthocyanin pigments (which give a wine its characteristic color), or the grapes' acidity level, which must be high enough for the wine to last for years and age well.

Château Kefraya is located in Lebanon, perhaps the world's oldest wine-producing region, three thousand feet above sea level. Libatel, a systems integrator, and Libelium teamed up to monitor the conditions using Libelium's wireless sensors to gather soil and climate information and how they affect the grapes.

Appropriately, the partners call the project "Precision Viticulture," and like other examples of the IoT mentioned previously, it's this precision that makes it so advantageous. The goals are to increase productivity and efficiency, improve quality for customers, and to adapt to global warming and other external changes.

Previously, this monitoring was all done by hand, expensive and time-consuming. Now, eight of Libelium's Waspmote Plug and Sense! Smart Agriculture PRO nodes do the work. Six of them are right at the grape level on the grapevine trunks, to report all the key variables critical to viticulture (temperature, humidity, and atmospheric pressure; solar radiation; soil humidity; soil temperature; and luminosity). One is next to the vineyard to combine the region's external weather conditions with the vineyard microclimate, and the last sensor is used for testing.[10]

Another example comes from marine fisheries, which are also heavily affected by global warming.

Oyster farming and harvesting has a particular need for realtime data, because oysters are "filter animals," ingesting contaminants that can result in serious human illnesses. Government agencies require constant testing of the oysters, and, if they fail, the oyster beds must be closed immediately. That decision is often triggered by rain forecasts, since rain can cause fertilizer or other runoffs that would contaminate the oysters. However, the weather data is often gathered a relatively long distance away, possibly making it inaccurate, and sometimes costing the farmers lost sales when a shutdown could have been avoided with accurate realtime data at the actual site.

In Tasmania, Bosch, which traditionally has concentrated on the auto industry, has invested in a startup, The Yield, focusing on agricultural IoT applications including oystering.

Using Bosch technology, including hardware, software, and realtime data management, measuring stations at the oyster banks calculate water depth and salinity, temperature, and atmospheric pressure, then algorithms interpret the data. The farmers can decide exactly when to harvest just by checking their smartphones, and—remember the "share data, don't hoard it" Essential Truth—government officials also get the data on a realtime basis, letting them reduce unnecessary closures by 30 percent while doing a better job of protecting public health. It's a win-win solution. Take that back: it's a win-win-win, because the realtime data is also shared with academic researchers studying oyster diseases.

IoT ImpactLABS is doing similar vineyard and oyster projects in Massachusetts.

GOVERNMENT

Government, too, is beginning to embrace the Internet of Things, with Barcelona being perhaps the outstanding example. As mentioned previously, businesses should get involved in these smart city efforts out of enlightened self-interest, especially since initiatives can have a major positive impact on corporate priorities such as improving deliveries and logistics through reductions in traffic and congestion.

Smart cities capitalize on the "share data, don't hoard it" Essential Truth, and nowhere is that more the case than Barcelona. The city began its IoT initiatives under former mayor Xavier Trius, who dramatically improved its infrastructure through the IoT. One example, again involving Libelium, was significantly reducing water usage in Poblenou Park Centre.[11]

New mayor Ada Colau puts equal emphasis on how the IoT can improve residents' quality of life and empower them. As her Chief Technology Officer and Digital Commissioner, Francesca Bria, says, her mandate is "to rethink the smart city from the ground up, meaning to rethink technology, [focusing] on what it can do to serve the people, instead of a technology push agenda." This is part of the new mayor's overall emphasis on participative democracy focusing on residents.

A key is sharing data, with its "Roadmap Toward Technological Sovereignty," to create an open-source common data infrastructure, with "an open-source sensor network, with common standards, connected to a computer platform managed by the city itself. Barcelona wants to retain ownership of its own network, platform, and data, and protect the data of its residents, yet ensure people and companies can access information that belongs in the public realm."[12]

This is reminiscent of work I did in 2008 as a consultant with District of Columbia CTO Vivek Kundra. He and Mayor Adrian Fenty opened up public access to more than forty important municipal databases on a realtime basis and then held the "Apps for Democracy" contest, open to everyone, to design apps capitalizing on the data in the public interest. The contest led to a range of valuable apps and spawned the global government open data movement.[13]

The Barcelona smart cities initiative is an important reminder that there should also be a qualitative aspect to IoT projects. It is very much a "high tech/high touch" approach, combining online projects with things such as face-to-face neighborhood planning meetings to create dialogue. "The city is enhancing its own transparency, inviting the public to flag any signs of corruption in municipal contracts it is putting online. It is also developing an online map and register of vacant properties and rentals as part of its drive to improve the supply of affordable housing. It hopes to encourage local small and medium-sized businesses to develop products and services using city networks and data."[14]

One example from Barcelona is in keeping with the BigBelly story from the beginning of the book. The city is taking one of the oldest, simplest parts of urban infrastructure, the streetlamp, and reinventing it as a key element not just in lighting, but also in a variety of other municipal services. Their electric consumption has been reduced by conversion to LEDs. Sensors detect when pedestrians are nearby and increase light levels to protect their safety. Equally important, the poles are like Christmas trees, hung with a variety of other important services:

- providing free internet access citywide
- using sensors to collect data on air quality, and share it with city agencies and the public[15]

In another example of "share data" thinking, Barcelona is working with an international group, CityProtocol, to create a common data-sharing standard. Yes, cities will still compete for new business and residents, but they have many needs in common, and access to easily shared databases will allow them to share best practices for the common good, especially as global warming forces them to place more emphasis on resilience.[16]

STARTUPS

Startups that embrace IoT strategies and technology in their projects from the beginning can fully capitalize on it and shed all of the klugy work-arounds that conventional devices had to include to minimize the effects of lack of realtime information and communication and micro-miniaturization of sensors.

Few things illustrate this better than two medical devices, the AliveCor Kardia heart monitor and the iQ handheld ultrasound.

AliveCor has for several years sold a small unit that sticks to the back of a smartphone, giving an FDA-approved EKG in precisely thirty seconds, simply by placing two fingers on each of the two panels and triggering the app. In practice, the Kardia can be more helpful than a $10,000 inpatient EKG, because patients can perform it on themselves while doing daily activities, annotate it ("just after workout," "after meditating"), and share it with their doctors, allowing their dosctors to know how their patients' heart functions in activities of daily living.[17]

The Kardia is a great example of the IoT at its best, because of the size, speed, and low cost, and because it extends the doctor-patient collaboration in a way that was simply impossible before the IoT. As the inventor and company CEO, Dr. David Albert, puts it, "Let's connect people directly to doctors. The straightest connection is a direct line."[18]

Demonstrating how the IoT can improve products' performance by adding elements of Artificial Intelligence, the company recently released a version mounted on the band of an Apple Watch ("KardiaBand and SmartRhythm monitoring"), combining the Kardia device with Artificial Intelligence models that interpret heart rate and activity data the Apple Watch gathers with its heart rate sensor and accelerometer. "It compares your heart rate and changes in your heart rate over time to what it expects from your minute-by-minute level of activity and gives you a graphical display of where your heart rate falls within the boundaries predicted by the neural network. When the network sees a pattern of heart rate and activity that it does not expect, it notifies you to take an EKG using the KardiaBand." Obviously, an inpatient test couldn't document this correlation between activity and heart rate—a clear advantage for the IoT device. Or, as Dr. Albert puts it, "Our technology suggests a future in which detection of heart arrhythmias can be non-invasive, ultra-convenient, and highly reliable."[19]

The second pure-play IoT medical device that shows how imaginative outsiders can reinvent a product through a combination of the IoT, the latest in manufacturing techniques, and Artificial Intelligence is the Butterfly iQ handheld ultrasound, which attaches to a smartphone, uses the phone's display rather than requiring a dedicated display, and fits in a pants pocket. The FDA has already approved the iQ for diagnosis in thirteen applications.

Proof of the pudding? The physician who invented it used the Butterfly iQ to diagnose his own cancer in time for surgery and cure.

The economic argument for the Butterfly iQ is convincing. As the marketing pitch goes, "Whole body imaging. Under $2K." (That's as opposed to $115,000 for the average conventional machine.)

The video on the startup's website shows the physicians trying it seem truly amazed by its versatility and ease-of-use—not to mention it can be accessed instantly in a life-or-death situation and operated by a non-expert. As one doctor said, "This blows up the entire ultrasound playing field."[20]

Underscoring the potential for revolutionary change by a company unencumbered by any purely physical device heritage, the Butterfly uses a single probe instead of the three on conventional ultrasound machines and can document conditions located from the superficial to deep inside the body. The entire bulky ultrasound machine is reduced to a far-less-costly chip (including a lot of signal processing and computational power) and capitalizes on technologies developed for consumer electronics. The approach doesn't just equal the traditional piezioelectric technology, but surpasses it, with power that would cost more than $100,000 with a conventional machine. Butterfly can use the same chip machines used to produce consumer goods such as smartphones and can print nearly a hundred ultrasound systems on less than one disk.

As incredible as the iQ's impact will be in the U.S., think of its potential to bring ultrasound to developing nations worldwide for the first time, where the cost and difficulty of transporting a bulky, sensitive system are impossible obstacles.

Finally, demonstrating the ease of grafting emerging technologies on the IoT, the Butterfly's Artificial Intelligence will guide even inexperienced personnel to do high-quality imaging within a few seconds![21]

ALEXA, WHAT'S THE IoT?: THE IoT GETS PERSONAL

The Future Is Smart concentrates on corporate use of the IoT, primarily because estimates say that 70 percent of its benefits will be realized on a B2B basis.[22] Yet the consumer market is both important in its own right and because it may have indirect B2B effects. For instance, buying and using a personal IoT device may introduce senior managers in a wide range of industries to the IoT, just as buying holiday gifts on Amazon in the 1990s introduced many of their counterparts to the potential profits from e-commerce. The experience may give them the courage to experiment with the IoT in their own enterprises. Finally, wouldn't it be ridiculous to totally revolutionize your production and operations but still churn out the same old products?

Redesigning existing products and services for the IoT and creating new ones won't be easy, largely because we have no past history for merging the physical and digital. It requires a new mind-set and a new skill set. You will need to find creative ways to seamlessly integrate the digital and physical and create user experiences that go beyond those possible with merely physical products. This is also a strong argument for the Circular Company vision that will be the focus of Chapter 8, because designing IoT products requires equal parts electronics and physical product design skills.

One of the experts on this issue is MIT Media Lab guru David Rose, author of the charming and insightful *Enchanted Objects: Design, Human Desire, and the Internet of Things*. Rose is not afraid of getting his hands dirty either, as he is the inventor of the Vitality GloCap IoT pill reminder system.

In his book, Rose argues that companies that want to capitalize on the IoT must eschew frivolous devices (the L'Oréal smart hairbrush comes to mind. Is this really needed?) and instead "fundamentally start with human desire in its most basic forms. In doing so they can focus on creating products that can have a meaningful and positive impact in the world."[23]

To meet this standard, Rose details six categories—providing a handy set of criteria by which to evaluate any consumer IoT device you're contemplating. Here's a summary:

1. Omniscience: "We have a voracious appetite to know as much as possible and to know about things that go beyond facts and information."

2. Telepathy: "We have a powerful desire to connect to the thoughts and feelings of others, and to be able to communicate with ease, richness, and transparency."

3. Safekeeping: "To feel comfortable, safe, and at ease."

4. Immortality: "We dream of living long lives, vital to the last moment."

5. Teleportation: "To live unconstrained by physical limits or boundaries."

6. Expression: "We all wish to be generative, to fully express ourselves in many forms and media."[24]

Rose says that the emergence of "Enchanted Objects" meeting these deeply felt human needs will begin with ordinary physical objects that we take for granted, from light bulbs to toothbrushes. "The ordinary thing is then augmented and enhanced through the use of emerging technologies: sensors, actuators, wireless connection, and embedded processing, so that it becomes extraordinary. The enchanted object then gains some remarkable power or ability that makes it more useful, more delightful, more informative, more sensate, more connected, more engaging, than its ordinary self."[25]

It's critical in designing IoT devices for the consumer market to remember that a major part of why people buy, use, and frequently love these products is that they are so personal. We entrust them with personal data about our lives, and that carries a heavy burden of responsibility. Make certain that Essential Truth #1, *make privacy and security your top priority,* is uppermost in mind. As explained in Chapter 3, once public confidence in your product is lost because of a privacy or security breach, it is hard to regain.

At the time of this writing, the running app Strava had been hit by just such a breach: the locations of hidden U.S. military bases around the world were potentially revealed because servicepeople were among those using the app. Their exercise paths, mapped by the company, showed the previously unknown locations.[26] You can imagine my sense of dread as the father of a military officer who has served in some of these locations.

The company may have thought it offered sufficient protections by anonymizing individuals' data, but it made a major privacy gaffe because it required users to opt out of having their path reported, rather than opting in if they did want it tracked. (Opting in should be the *de facto* standard for any app resulting in sharing of personal data.)

At the same time, the Strava situation illustrates exactly how challenging the privacy and security protection requirement is: Prior to this disclosure, who could have expected such a strange potential problem? The Strava incident threatened every other IoT device manufacturer, simply due to the ancient principle of guilt by association. Fair? No. True? Yes.

The ultimate lesson from the Strava debacle? This is a never-ending struggle: You must take *every* reasonable privacy and security measure from the beginning and then *constantly* revisit them. Think like a brilliant, deranged bad guy to brainstorm the wackiest possible threats and ways to thwart them—then upgrade your protections.

This is yet another argument for the Circular Company concept to be detailed in Chapter 8, because the more diverse the group charged with constantly reevaluating your protections, the more likely they are to discover flaws that none of them would have thought of working in isolation.

IoT DESIGN MANIFESTO

One of the most thoughtful perspectives on responsible design of IoT devices comes from a global collaborative that has created what it called the "IoT Design Manifesto 1.0," subtitled "Guidelines for responsible design in a connected world." It's pithy and provocative, worth repeating in its entirety, and very much in line with the Essential Truths discussed earlier. *Commit it to memory*:

1. **We don't believe the hype.** We pledge to be skeptical of the cult of the new—just slapping the internet onto a product isn't the answer. Monetizing only through connectivity rarely guarantees sustainable commercial success.

2. **We design useful things.** Value comes from products that are purposeful. Our commitment is to design products that have a meaningful impact on people's lives; IoT technologies are merely tools to enable that.

3. **We aim for the win-win-win.** A complex web of stakeholders is forming around IoT products: from users, to businesses, and everyone in between. We design so that there is a win for everybody in this elaborate exchange.

4. **We keep everyone and everything secure.** With connectivity comes the potential for external security threats executed through the product itself, which comes with serious consequences. We are committed to protecting our users from these dangers, whatever they may be.

5. **We build and promote a culture of privacy.** Equally severe threats can also come from within. Trust is violated when personal information gathered by the product is handled carelessly. We build and promote a culture of integrity where the norm is to handle data with care.

6. **We are deliberate about what data we collect.** This is not the business of hoarding data; we only collect data that serves the utility of the product and service. Therefore, identifying what those data points are must be conscientious and deliberate.

7. **We make the parties associated with an IoT product explicit.** IoT products are uniquely connected, making the flow of information among stakeholders open and fluid. This results in a complex, ambiguous, and invisible network. Our responsibility is to make the dynamics among those parties more visible and understandable to everyone.

8. **We empower users to be the masters of their own domain.** Users often do not have control over their role within the network of stakeholders surrounding an IoT product. We believe that users should be empowered to set the boundaries of how their data is accessed and how they are engaged with via the product.

9. **We design things for their lifetime.** Currently, physical products and digital services tend to be built to have different lifespans. In an IoT product, features are codependent, so lifespans need to be aligned. We design products and their services to be bound as a single, durable entity.

10. **In the end, we are human beings.** Design is an impactful act. With our work, we have the power to affect relationships between people and technology, as well as among people. We don't use this influence to only make profits or create robot overlords; instead, it is our responsibility to use design to help people, communities, and societies thrive.[27]

Combined, these ten points aren't just a lofty statement of principles, but also a very practical framework to create the kind of win-win-win devices the members aim for. Some developers who lose sight of these principles create devices that fall into the "just because you can make it doesn't mean you should make it" category: the IoT versions don't justify the expense because they don't substantially improve on the old, "dumb" device. Limiting data collection to what's really vital and then protecting that data reduces your exposure—and doesn't needlessly add to the volume of data you'll be collecting. Users want to control and customize their devices. All in all, the manifesto is a smart working guide to IoT device design.

AMAZON ECHO, THE BREAKTHROUGH IoT DEVICE

Any discussion of IoT consumer devices must start with *the* IoT phenomenon: the Amazon Echo, and its "voice," Alexa.

First released (by invitation only) in 2014, the Echo and its smaller variants, the Spots, etc., have become bestsellers, jumping to more than 5 million in sales in 2016, then quadrupling, to more than 20 million in 2017.[28]

The devices became more and more capable during the same period, not only because of technical advances, but because Amazon really gets the "share data, don't hoard it" Essential Truth. Specifically, there has been an explosion in the number of "skills" (Amazon's term for the apps developed using its Smart Home Skill API kit) from third-party developers to capitalize on Alexa and her capabilities. Amazon's Alexa Voice Service developer program lets other companies build their own Alexa devices—and each new one makes the others more valuable because of the "network effects" phenomenon.

As Amazon chair Jeff Bezos said in announcing Q4 2017 results, "There are now over 30,000 skills from outside developers, customers can control more than 4,000 smart home devices from 1,200 unique brands with Alexa, and we're seeing strong response to our new far-field voice kit for manufacturers."[29]

As anyone who uses an Echo device can tell you, Alexa's appeal comes from the near-flawless way it understands and responds to your commands, using the most universal and simplest input, the human voice. You don't have to find a device and then open an app, but simply speak. Through AI, the more you talk to Alexa, the better it responds to your particular speech, vocabulary, and preferences.

Yes, there have been fears that the Echo may be recording your voice all the time, making you vulnerable to privacy assaults, but so far there have been no substantiated cases where this has happened.

I have written elsewhere that the Echo could be the key to my vision of "SmartAging," combining smart health devices that can help seniors stay healthy longer with smart home devices that make it easier to manage a home as you age. The overall goal is to keep seniors healthy longer and out of institutions. The Echo, by using a simple voice input, lets tech-averse seniors realize all of its benefits without having to actually learn how to program and run the device.[30]

ALPHABET'S NEST

Another area of life that resisted digitization in the past was the home. All of our devices and appliances were mechanical, required hands-on attention to regulate them, and their internal operations were inscrutable. This led to problems such as frozen pipes in vacation homes when there was a sudden cold snap during the off-season or being forced to make a Hobson's choice: waste money and energy by leaving lights on when you were at work or come home to a dark home in the evening. Not to mention frustration on utilities' part about not being able to manage load during hot summer days, so that they had to use their oldest, least-efficient, and most-polluting generating facilities. "Smart home" devices now make remote control of individual devices possible, as well as allowing a single action to regulate several devices simultaneously. For instance, a command to Apple's HomeKit that "it's time for bed," might simultaneously turn off the Hue lights, turn down the Ecobee thermostat, and engage the Schlage lock.

While its sales are a small fraction of the Echo's, one of the first high-profile IoT consumer devices, the Nest smart thermostat (introduced in 2011), provides a good example of the IoT's multiple benefits. While it comes with a phone app to control the thermostat when you're away from home (checking on the house temperature during an unexpected freeze, turning up the temperature when you're returning home from work ahead of your schedule, etc.), most of the programming is done through sensors that monitor your occupancy patterns during the first weeks after installation and then automatically program the device through Artificial Intelligence.

The results are staggering. Nests have saved users billions of kWh of energy, an average of 10 to 12 percent on heating bills, and 15 percent on cooling.[31] The physical design is elegant, and installation is amazingly user-friendly. Early in 2018, Nest announced a lower-cost, less glamorous version. In cooperation with utilities, government agencies, and nonprofits, they are installing a million of that version in low-income people's homes. The idea is to address what's called "fuel poverty," a kind of hidden tax affecting poorer people typically living in less-insulated homes, with less-efficient furnaces, translating into "a median energy burden of 7.2 percent, compared to 2.3 percent of higher-income households in those areas."[32] Nest's initiative represents another example of the IoT Design Manifesto's win-win-win objective.

Even more impressive, Nest seems to epitomize the "share data, don't hoard it" IoT Essential Truth. Within the company itself, Nest has diversified into complementary devices such as smoke alarms and detection cameras that work together. Each becomes more valuable as a result. For example, the Next Protect smoke alarm links to the Nest thermostat, which turns off the heating system if it detects smoke, so that the problem doesn't become worse.

Equally important (if the homeowners opt in), Nest will provide anonymized data from the devices to partnering companies, resulting in another form of win-win-win. The smoke alarm data can result in a lower home insurance premium for the homeowner, while providing data to the electric or gas utility makes their home part of smart grid efforts. Reducing electric use during peak demand via the Nest's "Rush Hour Rewards" can result in a payment to the owner while the utility may be able to avoid cranking up its "peaking" units—the oldest, most inefficient, and most polluting ones. The third winner? The global environment, since these programs reduce global warming.[33]

For three years, Nest was a subsidiary of Google's parent company, Alphabet. In early 2018, it was brought back into Google as part of its hardware division, to maximize synergies with other Google hardware projects such as Google Home through Google's initiatives in machine learning and AI.[34]

Smart home devices such as the Nest are excellent examples of how the IoT can take formerly purely mechanical processes to run a home, from thermostats to lights, and turn them into the digital-physical merger that eliminates waste, increases comfort, and produces customer loyalty.

APPLE WATCH

You may remember that GE's Bill Ruh predicted that every person might someday have a digital twin from birth to help with their healthcare, making it possible to do predictive maintenance on our bodies. The Kardia iPhone attachment described previously is a first step in that direction. As the inventor, Dr. David Albert, told me, his vision was to "connect people directly to doctors, because the straightest connection is a direct line."[35]

Whether it's to goad ourselves to increase our fitness or to bring to light and detail previously unknown health conditions, a key to that kind of accurate realtime reporting on our bodies is wearable devices. The best-selling of those is the Apple Watch, which not only combines health and fitness functions, but also personal productivity and entertainment (including the critical ability to send emojis in response to a message, LOL!). It can even tell time. No wonder the watch is frequently referred to as Apple's most personal product: much of its value comes from harvesting, relaying, and analyzing data about the wearer.[36]

One of the keys to the watch's versatility is the combination of four sophisticated sensors on the back. They allow the creation of very accurate algorithms to track more than twenty specific fitness activities, from outdoor runs to indoor walks, rowing machines to ellipticals. Once again applying the "share data, don't hoard it" Essential Truth, Apple has reached out since the first Apple Watch to encourage more apps from independent developers that capitalize on the constant data stream from the watch, including prestigious medical institutions such as Stanford.

As with so many other IoT devices, the fact that the data flow is constant, and in realtime, allows for design of apps that can let users (and, in some cases, their healthcare providers) know instantly about important body changes in time to act on the information. Yes, after-the-fact information is still valuable, but being able to act on it immediately is far more important, one of the reasons why the Apple Watch displays key daily activity data as three concentric circles. One of the most memorable examples came soon after the watch's introduction, when a high school football player in a Boston suburb felt funny during a practice and got an alert from his watch about an abnormally high heart rate, just in time to seek emergency care—his heart, liver, and kidneys were shutting down due to a rare condition.[37]

In early 2018, an app company called Cardiogram announced that its app, developed in collaboration with the University of California, San Francisco, and using the company's DeepHeart neural network, was 85 percent accurate at distinguishing between those who have and don't have diabetes. This was significant because it showed it was possible to analyze a continuous stream of data from users, which uncovered a previously unknown correlation. This volume of data—more than 200 million sensor measurements of resting heart rate and heart rate variability from 14,011 individual hearts in their daily routines—could never have been gathered and analyzed until the advent of wearables. Early detection of diabetes can lead to earlier intervention and less-severe illness (think predictive maintenance with the jet turbines, a strikingly similar pattern).[38] Similarly, people who can easily visualize their physical activity (or lack thereof if they haven't closed the circles on the watch) may become motivated to exercise more frequently and for longer periods of time.

HUE LIGHTS

Along with the Nest thermostat, the other early smart home device that has become mainstream is the Philips Hue LED light bulb, introduced in 2012.

In addition to one bulb that just shows white light, there is another with three elements that is capable of 16 *million* different color combinations. It communicates with other bulbs and the control hub via the Zigbee protocol; newer models can be controlled by the Apple HomeKit platform.

Philips said at the time the Hue bulbs were introduced that it would release the API used to create controls for the bulb and did so in early 2013. According to systems architect George Yianni, "We actually want to help and grow and encourage this community and give them tools and proper documentation. Also, we want to give them commitment that this is the API and we're going to support it and it won't change overnight."[39] Using this API, the Hue became one of the most popular devices on the do-it-yourself IFTTT site mentioned previously, with users creating IFTTT "recipes" for everything from best light for concentration (by a group of neurologists) to "Wake to the colors of roses on Valentine's Day!"[40]

However, opening up the API was not without its risks. In 2016, a team of Canadian and Israeli ethical hackers showed how a mesh network of the bulbs could be hacked to create a "citywide bricking event" in which hackers took over the system in an urban area to create havoc. Representatives from Philips claim that they addressed the concern with a security update.[41]

Despite their diversity—from the Echo to thermostats to watches to light bulbs—these consumer IoT devices illustrate striking similarities to what we've seen previously with industrial IoT devices:

- The greater impact possible when the data streams are opened and shared, because of the network effects phenomenon
- The ability to lift the Collective Blindness obstacles that kept us from understanding phenomena before we could gather and analyze realtime data
- The new ability to take preventive measures to minimize problems and their effects if they can be documented when in their earliest stages

This pattern indicates that we will be able to develop more robust and effective IoT devices and practices in the future when these approaches and the Essential Truths underlying them become commonplace as the shift to IoT thinking becomes routine.

While components of the IoT (especially emerging ones such as virtual reality and Artificial Intelligence) will continue to evolve and become less expensive, all the components of a viable IoT strategy are already available, particularly if you begin your journey with an emphasis on using the IoT to improve the precision of what you already make and how you make it. Building on the bottom-line savings from that phase, you can begin to use many of the same components for more fundamental change in every aspect of your organization, as we will see in the next chapter.

SELF-ASSESSMENT

1. Do the examples in this chapter help to ease your fears about the difficulty of beginning to make the IoT transition?

2. What areas of your current operations are hampered, and costs increased, by lack of actionable realtime data about your manufacturing processes, maintenance, and product design? How would realtime data on those factors improve your precision and reduce costs?

3. Did the examples of IoT-based startups make you realize how your own products could be fundamentally reinvented by the IoT? What are the risks to your competitive position for not exploring similar transitions with your products?

PART III: **AFTER THE REVOLUTION**

7

The IoT Snowball

Packing It All Together

The prior chapters provided examples on how the IoT is already providing important benefits to companies and customers alike, even in its early days and with only partial implementation.

However, what has happened to date only provides a fragmentary glimpse of the breathtaking transformation that will happen when IoT thinking (i.e., fully embracing and internalizing the four IoT Essential Truths) becomes commonplace, key components such as sensors and platforms become robust and fully affordable, and network effects become commonplace in the IoT. Devices will still be physical. They will be equally digital. They will have incredible capabilities.

This chapter describes what will happen when this merger is fully realized. It looks at the strategies of companies that have already achieved significant transformation, often because they are either startups unhampered by Collective Blindness or because a previous inability to see every aspect of a product's lifecycle caused their company or their customers unacceptable levels of risk.

For our purposes, we will use the name for IoT products that Michael Porter and James Heppelmann coined in their seminal HBR series on the IoT: "smart, connected devices." That's about as succinct a description as we can find for smart products (and, for that matter, some services as well) because it gives equal emphasis to the physical and digital.[1]

So how will smart, connected devices be designed, built, marketed, used, and maintained? From a strategic and financial standpoint, it makes the most sense to begin by increasing the efficiency of your current operations through more precise manufacturing, then applying the savings to the more sweeping and difficult to implement areas of product design and maintenance.

However, it is absolutely essential to understand that the most revolutionary aspect of the IoT company of the future will be that there won't be a neat, linear procession from one of these factors to the next, and you won't pursue discrete strategies for each of them. Every aspect will be inextricably linked at every step. A never-ending circle will come about from the seamless merger of the physical and digital.

It might be best to visualize the result as a snowball that continually grows in size as it rolls down a hill, gaining momentum and size from each addition to the IoT complex. Most of the examples that follow reflect multiple and diverse benefits. That's the essence of the IoT: melding the physical and digital makes individual examples a microcosm of the entire IoT.

PRECISION

Of all the components of IoT-based business, the one that's already most advanced is the increase in manufacturing precision, with the beacon being Siemens 99.9985 percent quality rate at the "Factory of the Future." Imagine what the economic and environmental effects would be if that rate became the norm in factories. Even before you improve your product design and maintenance, you will achieve bottom-line benefits from more efficient and precise manufacturing that you can then reinvest in these other areas. As you add each new component of an integrated approach, the benefits will snowball.

The concept of a transition to manufacturing that inextricably intertwines the physical and digital is not just in the products but in every aspect of the manufacturing process to create them, best embodied in the Industry 4.0 concept introduced by the German government in 2011 at the annual Hamburg Messe event.

It's a far cry from traditional manufacturing, where a delay or maintenance problem in one part of the assembly line could bring everything to a halt, and the best management could do was to track a relatively few performance indicators (usually after the fact) and adjust equipment manually. Given the process's complexity, any thought of really optimizing production efficiency and precision was laughable, let alone mass customization allowing customers real choice in terms of how their particular product was configured.

Today, that is no longer the case.

We might dismiss the Amberg plant as an aberration, since Siemens manufactures the sensors that are used to fine-tune operations, so of course they'd make it a showcase. However, that's not the case with Harley-Davidson's motorcycle plant in York, Pennsylvania, which was totally rebuilt in 2012 to incorporate IoT communication technology and smart assembly line units. The process replaced forty-one buildings with only two and won *Industry Week*'s 2013 "Best Plants" Award.[2] Among other changes in the totally wired factory, automated carts move parts around the assembly area, and the robots that weld the fenders turn out 20 percent more per shift than in the past, with fewer workers.

This is not a happily-ever-after story.

Employment at the York facility was more than two thousand in 2009, before the makeover. Despite labor concessions, only eight hundred work there now.[3] Since Harley had threatened to close the plant completely and move production overseas, the impact would have been even greater if the smart-manufacturing changes hadn't been made.

At the Daimler Trucks factory mentioned previously, factory operations before the IoT were marred by low quality, poor wireless coverage, and an inability to monitor and coordinate every part of the assembly line. The entire factory is now networked, which is essential because of the wide variety of customized trucks they build, with differing wheel bases, axles, colors, air cleaners, and other parts. The secret is a secure, plant-wide WiFi network that allows total coordination. Managers can check parts inventories in realtime on iPads, while plant workers also have the realtime access they need to customize individual trucks.

A key example of the links between all players with the IoT is that Daimler workers can quickly connect with vendors' experts if there is a problem with machinery, and predictive maintenance is possible because of the system's ability to easily identify all parts.

Similarly, SAP's Digital Manufacturing rapid-deployment solution provides intelligence on the shop floor, enables a batch size of one, supports the handover from engineering to manufacturing, and assures state-of-the-art production execution.[4]

Looking ahead, perhaps the best preview of what will be possible with the IoT in manufacturing comes from Local Motors. It combines the IoT with innovations such as 3-D printing and what the company calls "micromanufacturing." Its best-known accomplishment, creating the first 3-D printed vehicle, is only part of what it calls direct digital manufacturing (DDM), whose other benefits include:

- making parts directly from CAD files
- reducing tooling costs
- cutting time lag between design and production
- mass customization[5]

Local Motors does the manufacturing in what it calls "microfactories," which are designed for rapid prototyping, modular experimentation, and small-batch manufacturing.

Watch Local Motors carefully. Their direct digital manufacturing model, combined with the IoT, may turn out to be a viable and even dominant one for the twenty-first century: smaller, nimbler, and built around all the latest technologies.

Local Motors isn't alone in radically rethinking manufacturing, especially with regard to 3-D printing. As you may remember, GE is actively involved in the area, and HP and

Deloitte have created an "additive manufacturing alliance" around HP's new factory-grade 3-D printers.[6]

WHAT ABOUT THE FORGOTTEN WORKERS?

If we remember to ask the crucial "who else can use this data?" question, the benefits of smart manufacturing can and should be broadened to include both the supply chain and rank-and-file workers. There may be fewer workers on assembly lines today, but they are still crucial, especially because they have a long history of actually executing the designs. Why not empower them?

Osram has given every worker at its Berlin factory access to "Ticket Manager," an app on the workers' personal smart-phones giving them realtime data on the more than eight machines they must manage, improving operations.[7]

The most ambitious effort to empower factory-floor workers comes from a startup, Tulip. Its IoT gateway lets anyone add sensors, tools, cameras, and even "pick-to-light bins" (which light up sequentially to show workers the order in which to pick up pieces) to the workstation, without writing a line of code, because the software's diverse drivers support factory-floor devices. It claims to "fill the gap between rigid back-end man-ufacturing IT systems and the dynamic operations taking place on the shop floor."[8]

Tulip shows how the IoT can and must bring about previ-ously impossible-to-achieve precision in *every* aspect of busi-ness. Its features, especially the no-code, low-code aspect, demonstrate that the IoT will eventually empower everyone with tools that even those without special training can use to address their own specific needs.

Tulip cofounder Rony Kubat says people who actually have to play a hands-on role in product design and production on the shop floor have been ignored in the IoT, and many processes such as training are still paper-based:

> Manufacturing software needs to evolve. Legacy applications neglect the human side of manufacturing and therefore suffer from low adoption. The use of custom, expensive-to-maintain, in-house solutions is rampant. The inability of existing solutions to address the needs of people on the shop floor is driving the proliferation of paper-based workflows and the use of word processing, spreadsheet, and presentation applications as the mainstay of manufacturing operations. Tulip aims to change all this through our intuitive, people-centric platform. Our system makes it easy for manufacturers to connect hands-on work processes, machines and backend IT systems through flexible self-serve manufacturing apps.[9]

The startup has dozens of customers in fields as varied as medical devices, pharma, and aerospace. The results are dramatic and quite varied:

- **Quality.** A Deloitte analysis of Tulip's use at Jabil, a global contract manufacturer, documented greater than 10 percent production increases. It reduced quality issues in manual assembly by more than 10 percent. Production yield increased by more than 10 percent, and manual assembly quality issues were reduced by 60 percent in the initial four weeks of operation.[10]

- **Training.** Other customers reduced the amount of time to train new operators by 90 percent, in a highly complicated, customized, and regulated biopharmaceutical training situation: "Previously, the only way to train new operators was to walk them repeatedly through all the steps with an experienced operator and a process engineer. Tulip quickly deployed its software along with IoT gateways for the machines and devices on the process and managed to cut training time almost by half."[11]

- **Time to market.** They reduced a major athletic apparel maker's time to market by 50 percent for hundreds of new product variations. That required constantly evaluating the impact of dozens of different quality drivers to isolate the root causes of defects—including both manual and automated platforms. Before Tulip, it could take weeks of analysis until a process was ready for production. According to the quality engineer on the project, "I used Tulip's apps to communicate quality issues to upstream operators in realtime. This feedback loop enabled the operators to take immediate corrective action and prevent additional defects from occurring."[12]

The no-code, low-code aspect of Tulip's manufacturing app platform lets process engineers without programming backgrounds create shop-floor apps through interactive step-by-step work instructions. "The apps give you access through our cloud to an abundance of information and realtime analytics that can help you measure and fine-tune your manufacturing operations," Tulip cofounder Natan Linder says. No-code, low-code IoT software such as Tulip, Mendix, or Kony bear watching for IoT, because they democratize app design, empowering those with the greatest understanding of each company's specific needs: the end user.[13]

Linder looked at analytics apps that let users create apps through simple tools and thought—why not provide the same kinds of tools for training technicians on standard operating procedures or for building product or tracking quality defects? "This is a self-service tool that a process or quality engineer can use to build apps. They can create sophisticated workflows without writing code. . . . Our cloud authoring environment basically allows you to just drag and drop and connect all the different faucets and links to create a sophisticated app in minutes, and deploy it to the floor, without writing code," he says. Tulip enables sharing appropriate realtime analytics with each team member no matter where they are and setting up personal alerts for the data that's relevant to each.[14]

Although often overlooked, the benefits of empowering shop-floor workers through the IoT are potentially huge. According to the *UK Telegraph*, output can increase 8 to 9 percent, while cutting costs 7 to 8 percent. The same research estimates that industrial companies "could see as much as a 300 basis point boost to their bottom line."[15]

IDC analyst John Santagate neatly sums up the argument for empowering workers through the IoT:

With all of the talk and concern around the risk of losing the human element in manufacturing, due to the increasing use of robotics, it is refreshing to see a company focus on improving the work that is still done by human hands. We typically hear the value proposition of deploying robots and automation of improvements to efficiency, quality, and consistency. But what if you could achieve these improvements to your manufacturing process by simply applying analytics and technology to the human effort? This is exactly what they are working on at Tulip. . . .

We don't often think about digital transformation in relation to human effort, but this is exactly the sort of thinking that can deliver some of the early wins in digital transformation.[16]

An important subtheme of the IoT, based on "share data, don't hoard it," is empowering everyone involved through data, not just a few elites. I developed this theme in my earlier book, *Data Dynamite,* and which, ironically, led me to the IoT.[17] Santagate's insights might well be applied to others in the IoT value chain, such as retailers and end users. Libellium CEO Asín told me that she thinks the next stage in the IoT will be when subject matter experts, not just data analysts, become comfortable working with IoT data as a way to build their professional clout.[18]

CYCLICAL DESIGN

Once we're manufacturing more efficiently, we need to manufacture different things: those smart, connected devices. These devices will certainly be physical, but designers will include inextricably linked digital components from the get-go, rather than as an afterthought.

A prime example is the Butterfly IQ for performing ultrasounds, discussed in a previous chapter. The design is disruptive: a system that once required a heavy, bulky, and complex physical product is reduced to an integrated chip small enough to fit in a pocket. The chip includes more than nine thousand tiny drums that wobble to create sounds, then receive the response from the body—a tiny fraction of the size that would be required with a mechanical equivalent. (It also allows the ultrasound to be done with a single probe, rather than the three that are required on conventional machines.) The chip comes with other benefits as well:

- It can be printed on the same machines used to print consumer electronic chips, bringing down the price.
- Because it's electronic, it can be designed to have much greater bandwidth than a traditional piezo-electric transducer could.
- The chip also includes signal processing and computational power, reducing the need for outside equipment to process the results, and allowing effects that would otherwise only be possible with an extremely expensive machine.

Even more clever, it dispenses with a dedicated display, because we all carry an excellent one in our pockets: our smartphones!

The company's website speaks to the potential for transformation possible not only with this device, but also when we apply the same synergistic thinking to all products in the near future: "Our dream becomes reality at the intersection of semi-conductor engineering, artificial intelligence, and the cloud." Think how these design components would liberate your product's size, versatility, choice of materials, and cost.

The digital-physical merger means that a concept from software design, the user experience, becomes more important to products and a new challenge for designers. As with app design, this may mean that you can design in a variety of possible ways to allow the end user to choose how it works depending on user preferences (think of the user-adjustable settings on your smartphone), rather than having to design for a single common-denominator user (which probably meant that it didn't really fit any individual's exact choices!). That also means the end user can actually play an important role in determining how the product actually feels and works. John Deere, for example, used to manufacture several different engines for their tractors. Now the customer can choose which horsepower option to use from a single, standard engine by just pressing a button.[19]

It will be crucial to consider how the end user will interact with IoT products.

As one design consultancy said, it actually can get down to the level of building in "conversational empathy" with the user.[20] Anyone who has had to deal with voice-activated assistants that just don't seem to understand you can sympathize with that request. But imagine how hard it will be for engineers, who never had to wrestle with such touchy-feely issues, to address yet another design choice, especially one that's so hard to quantify.

While the products will still be physical in form, more of what differentiates them will be digital, because that is what allows flexibility in actual use—and customer delight.

Design has taken place in a vacuum in the past, in a design studio isolated from the reality of how the customer actually uses the product in the field (in cases such as tractors, literally in a field). At best, companies used tools such as focus groups and surveys to *try* to learn what customers might want, with social media added into the mix in recent years. With the IoT, as Eric Gervet of A.T. Kearney has said, there will be a paradigm shift in product design, away from the product in isolation to how the customer actually uses it, because we can now learn firsthand from the product:

> "Experience is now the product," said Gervet. Experience, he added, is co-created between the product and the user. "You create your own experience, which is why it matters so much to you," he said. And good or bad memories are all about the experience.[21]

As mentioned previously, GE has already made the switch to iterative design based on constant feedback from the digital twin. VP of Global Software William Ruh reports that:

> GE is adopting practices like releasing stripped-down products quickly, monitoring usage, and rapidly changing designs depending on how things are used by customers. These approaches follow the "lean startup" style at many software-intensive internet companies.

"We're getting these offerings done in three, six, nine months," he said. "It used to take three years."[22]

Merging the digital and physical can also create customer delight. Think, for example, of how you'd feel if you were heading north for a ski weekend and, instead of rushing to turn up the thermostat in the freezing lodge when you get there, you were welcomed instead by a toasty warm house, because you could turn the heat up from your car three hours earlier.

Perhaps the most productive design strategy will emerge from thinking of design as a continuous process, with accompanying changes in how your company will actually make money. Kearney's Suketu Gandhi noted "where pricing today is based on initial cost, pricing of the future will be based on calculating the *lifetime value of the product.*"[23]

For example, if you do make continual, incremental improvements, some physical and some through software, your new product sales may decrease and you may find it more profitable to switch to a product as service model. When that happens, customers may find that the data created by the product's operations may let them become far more efficient. They will be able to count on continuous operation without unexpected and costly shutdowns for major repairs, because sensor data will alert your company to the earliest onset of problems, in time to intervene and make less costly repairs (or even substitute upgraded parts) when there's a lull in their normal production schedules. Customers will become increasingly loyal, and less likely to switch to another manufacturer, because their needs will be continually assessed and met. (This concept will be treated in detail later in this chapter.)

One brash startup that we discussed for other reasons earlier in this chapter may point the way toward merged physical-digital design. Remember Local Motors, whose tag line is "We are focused on low volume manufacturing of open-source vehicle designs, using multiple microfactories and a co-creation SaaS platform." This is not your grandfather's GM!

Their first product, the Olli "self-driving cognitive" shuttle, was produced with a boost from IBM's Watson AI brainpower, but the company makes clear that its origins are also rooted in collaboration ("co-creation") between the company and users: what it calls its "community." Local Motors puts its money where its mouth is by sponsoring paid contests to solicit and reward the best ideas from the global public on how to further evolve the Olli to serve the specific needs of the aging and disabled.

To create these new hybrid physical/digital products, you'll need both engineers and software designers involved and working collaboratively from the earliest stages of design—in fact, Heppelmann and Porter predicted that design teams will shift toward more electrical engineers than mechanical ones.[24] Kearney's Gervet predicts that product design leadership may evolve into new roles: "A product officer, who will focus on designing innovative products, an experience officer, who will focus on designing innovative user experiences, and a data equity officer, who will focus on monetizing data."[25]

DESIGN THINKING

The new design philosophy required to fully capitalize on the IoT is a concept described in 2003, before the IoT was really viable, by David Kelly of IDEO, the legendary design studio. He called it "design thinking," and as summarized by Kaan Turnali, its principles were uncannily like the IoT:

- "Success comes from designing integrated solutions in which each part completes the system in whole—not designing fragmented pieces that make up a stack."
- "By getting closer to current or potential users and going beyond distant observation, we have a chance to design by looking out from the inside—rather than outside in."
- "Empathy opens up nerve endings so we can feel what it is like to be in another's shoes—a prerequisite for customer-centric design. We need to get as frustrated as the users/customers so we can better understand the pain points."
- "By bringing multidisciplinary teams together at the table, we leverage the power of collective expertise."
- "Embracing ambiguity allows us to seek new ideas we would otherwise miss. Embracing ambiguity opens the door for human ingenuity—allowing us to chase opportunities for new ideas we would otherwise miss."
- "Promoting the philosophy of 'fail early and often' is the key to harnessing the power of rapid prototypes and delivering proof of concepts that resonate and encourage feedback from actual users and customers."[26]

IoT devices will think. They will delight. They will be profitable.

SUPPLY CHAINS, DISTRIBUTION, AND SALES

Systems thinking guru Peter Senge used to run an exercise in his seminars to illustrate the problems that festered when various corporate functions operated in isolation from each other. The participants broke into teams divided by their functions, and planned their operations in isolation, or with only limited information about what others were doing. In one particularly memorable exercise, the manufacturing team ramped up for full-scale production based on rosy sales predictions, only to fill the warehouses with unsold products when new market conditions undercut the estimates.

Oops. Supply chains and distribution networks may not be glamorous, but they're essential, and the IoT can create an unprecedented degree of precision in what until now has been notoriously inefficient. You will have the option of sharing real-time production data with them that can improve the efficiency of their work.

Jeremy Rifkin, in his *The Zero Marginal Cost Society*, cited the work of Benoit Montreuil, the "Coca-Cola Material Handling & Distribution Chair and Professor" at Georgia Tech.

According to Rifkin, Montreuil calls for a "physical internet" for logistics, which he says is a necessity not only because of the environmental impacts of the current, inefficient system (such as 14 percent of all greenhouse gas emissions in France), but also its ridiculous costs, accounting for 10 percent of the U.S. GDP according to a 2009 Department of Transportation report.

Rifkin cites a variety of examples of the current system's inefficiency based on Montreuil's research:

- Trucks in the U.S. are, on average, only 60 percent full, and were empty for 20 percent of miles driven. Globally the efficiency is only 10 percent.
- U.S. business inventories were $1.6 trillion as of March 2013—so much for just-in-time.
- Time-sensitive products such as food, clothes, and medical supplies are unsold because they can't be delivered on time.

Montreuil's "physical internet" has striking parallels to the electronic one:

- Cargo (like packets) must be packaged in standardized module containers.
- Like the internet, the cargo must be structured independently of the equipment, so it can be processed seamlessly through a wide range of networks, with smart tags and sensors for identification and sorting.

Under the new system Montreuil visualized, the current warehouse and distribution mess would be replaced by a fully integrated one involving all of the 535,000 facilities nationwide, cutting time and dramatically reducing environmental impacts and fuel consumption.

Rifkin wrote that, most important for companies, "Montreuil points out that an open supply network allows firms to reduce their lead time to near zero if their stock is distributed among some of the hundreds of distribution centers that are located near their final buyer market."[27]

As if making a full-fledged IoT transformation weren't already complex enough, remember that when it comes to supply chains, there's a major factor you can't control yourself, transportation. Companies with complex supply chains would also be wise to throw their support behind public-private partnerships designed to streamline traffic through a combination of smart vehicles and smart control systems, such as the Obama administration's Smart City Challenge, which focused on transportation innovations from the neighborhood to the interstates. Columbus, Ohio, won the challenge with a plan covering the full range of smart transportation innovations, coordinated by a central traffic signal and integrated transportation data system. It demonstrated exactly how diverse and far-reaching the benefits of a totally linked and creative transportation network could be, from better health to more efficient business. A few of the components included:

- Using analytics and improved first-mile-last-mile connections to public transportation to improve healthcare access in a neighborhood with high infant mortality.
- Using self-driving electric shuttles to connect a new bus rapid transit center to a retail district, to help residents find jobs and boost retail sales.
- Using connected vehicle technology on city vehicles and at intersections to optimize traffic flow and demonstrate safety applications.
- Using connected vehicle technology in the city's freight district, including automated truck platooning and

traffic signal management. Similarly, the city will work with freight operators on deploying sensors for parking availability.[28]

Near the city, the state of Ohio is adding a thirty-five-mile "Smart Mobility Corridor" on a four-lane, limited access highway. High-capacity fiber optic cable will give researchers and traffic monitors realtime access to data from embedded and wireless sensors to test smart transportation technologies. As with the Columbus initiative, the Smart Mobility Corridor will be a public-private partnership.[29]

As this transportation-distribution network example illustrates, the smartest IoT strategy is one that constantly explores the possibility for synergies based on collaboration, whether that is between various departments within your own company, with complementary governmental initiatives, or with your supply chain, distribution network, retailers, and customers. When you have mushrooming volumes of realtime data, sharing access to that data is guaranteed to lead to more benefits than if it remains in isolation.

SALES

Sales is yet another area of business in which previously simple devices have become strategic by adding smart technology. In this case it's the humble vending machine, neatly closing a historical loop. Some say the IoT's birth happened when Carnegie Mellon students attempted to put a Coke machine online so they could be sure to get a cold drink. Nestle, Pepsi, and Coke are all deploying smart vending machines combining sensors, communications, big data analysis, and AI to not only automate restocking and improve delivery efficiency but also improve their ability to meet customers' desires with customized offerings. According to Coke International CTO Jane Gilmour, the company has launched several IoT initiatives, with the main aims being to improve not only the delivery of products, but also the products themselves. Realtime data tells the company which machines are busiest. Incorporating new technologies, in this case facial recognition and contactless payments, they can tell which varieties sell the most.

Most significant as a model for other retailers are Coke's Freestyle vending machines, which contain 150 concentrates. Users can create their own custom drinks, improving their refreshment experience while cutting the company's costs because it doesn't have to bottle each variety. At the same time, data on the new custom blends can give Coke valuable information on possible new standard blends.[30]

As is frequently the case, a single IoT tool such as the Freestyle can serve marketing *and* another need as well. Take the increasing interest in blockchain by Walmart and others to streamline supply chains. According to a post in the *LoadDelivered* blog, there are a wide array of benefits to linking your resupply system to blockchain, which is done through IoT sensor data:

- "Recording the quantity and transfer of assets—like pallets, trailers, containers, etc.—as they move between supply chain nodes."
- "Tracking purchase orders, change orders, receipts, shipment notifications, or other trade-related documents."

- "Assigning or verifying certifications or certain properties of physical products; for example, determining if a food product is organic or fair trade."
- "Linking physical goods to serial numbers, bar codes, digital tags like RFID, etc."
- "Sharing information about manufacturing process, assembly, delivery, and maintenance of products with suppliers and vendors."[31]

That kind of information should be irresistible to companies compared to the relative inefficiency of today's supply chain. The benefits include transparency, ability to scale, security, and innovation.[32]

In yet another example of how IoT components can pay simultaneous benefits in widely varied parts of your business, blockchain can also be an effective marketing tool, especially with those customers who worry about the purity of the materials that their food is produced from, possible allergens, and how those producing the food are treated by their employers. Barilla, the pasta company, worked with Cisco and others to install the Safety for Food (S4F) platform. Customers can simply scan a QR code on the back of some pasta and sauce packages to easily get data on the *specific production batch*. Barilla can use the same data to streamline its supply chain, cutting costs. There's even a potential regulatory benefit: rapid documentation in the case of a food safety recall. An IoT win-win for all parties concerned![33]

CUSTOMER DELIGHT
AND PREDICTIVE MAINTENANCE

Finally, we come to perhaps the most dramatic difference between the IoT and business before it: customer support and satisfaction.

In the past, we simply had no idea what happened to products after they were sold:

- Did they delight customers, merely satisfy them, or disappoint them?
- Did they function as designed, or were there patterns of failure that infuriated customers and called for design changes in further models? Did their operation ever endanger users?
- Did they leave certain functions unaddressed that might have been answered by accessories?
- Were the directions hard to follow? Did they lead customers to operate the devices improperly?
- Did the devices require constant readjustment to function efficiently?
- Were they difficult to repair because of lack of information about exactly how and why they failed?

And on and on. After-the-sale was simply an information void, and it caused problems for customers and companies alike.

Today, that information void is filled, and the potential for positive change is astounding.

It begins with the potential for customers to become partners in the design process. Data is fed back to designers via the digital twin, who can now see patterns that suggest new upgrades or opportunities for entirely new products to fill gaps the designers would never have known existed without this data.

In particular, the integration of digital and physical means that customers can make choices because of software; they can take a generic product and customize it to their personal needs through their software preferences. As *IoT Agenda* reported, "Manufacturers can now offer customizable, upgradable products and services flowing from a single device. Customers can alter the function and the value delivered by IoT devices." No company has refined this process more than Tesla:

> Tesla owners were no longer constrained to wait for a new automobile to take advantage of new features, and Tesla proved to the modern world that a car is no longer a fixed object but an ever-changing, ever-customizable service that can be tailored on an ongoing basis with new capabilities of value to customers.[34]

The benefits for Tesla include new revenue streams from customers who opt for software upgrades that allow autonomous driving, differentiating its cars from all others by this ability to add new functions instantly, "minimized manufacturing costs by offering this functionality via software rather than requiring the development of a new physical hardware model," and creating a direct and continuing personal relationship with every customer.[35] As we've seen with every other phase of the IoT, this interweaving of design, manufacturing, service, and marketing advances, which were simply impossible before the digital and physical were merged, requires an entirely new way of looking at business.

Maintenance used to be one of those necessary corporate evils, and a department where you might put, how shall we say it, some of your less creative thinkers. It was a drag on the bottom line, and frankly planning and budgeting could be a mystery. What would break next, and why? Since you wouldn't know what happened until after the fact, it was hard to deduce the causes. Since it usually left your customer without a usable product, often at a critical time, it meant customers were often angry—and that meant the next time they were in the market, they might defect to another company's products. It was also difficult to plan for manpower and supplies.

A typical strategy was to do scheduled maintenance, which usually involved picking a conservative estimate of when something might break and then requiring that the customer schedule the service, which they might fail to do. In other words, it was a guesstimate.

With the IoT, that's changing. As the headline on one report about predictive maintenance read, "Maintenance is increasingly seen as a strategic business function as opposed to a necessary evil."[36]

As with several previously cited aspects of the IoT, a good place to start to look for cutting-edge, well-planned predictive maintenance plans is in instances where failure isn't an option because of a combination of unacceptable economic, environmental, and loss-of-human-life consequences. In other words, on an offshore oil rig.

Forget for a moment the catastrophic human, environmental, and economic costs of a rig's failure, and just think about the practical ones: Rigs are located miles offshore, and due to size limits, can only keep a limited supply of spare parts on hand. If there is a serious problem, specialists may need to be rounded up, parts must be delivered to a staging area, then everything helicoptered to the scene. It's hard to think of any situation in which predictive maintenance could be more valuable. Oh, and don't forget that much of the critical equipment isn't on the rig at all but at the ocean floor, fifteen hundred feet or more below the platform, so direct inspection is difficult and dangerous.

There are powerful economic incentives to implement predictive maintenance, as well: the highly volatile oil market, especially with the added competition from fracked natural gas, has been hurt in recent years, in part due to falling efficiency. According to McKinsey, "Research shows that average production efficiency dropped in the past decade, while the performance gap between industry leaders and other companies widened, from 22 percentage points in 2000 to around 40 percentage points in 2012."[37]

With predictive maintenance, all major components of the rig are fitted with sensors to gather data about operations and the components' condition. According to a McKinsey study, a rig may have as many as 40,000 sensors—although much of the data went unanalyzed until the advent of big data analysis tools.[38]

Industrywide, the stakes are high for predictive maintenance. The U.S. Department of Energy reports that predictive maintenance programs in the oil and gas industry on average:

- Yield a tenfold return on investment
- Reduce maintenance costs 25 to 30 percent
- Eliminate 70 to 75 percent of breakdowns
- Reduce downtime 35 to 45 percent
- Increase production 20 to 25 percent[39]

Dynogram, which provides IoT services for a wide variety of customers in industry, retail, logistics, and manufacturing, created an IoT solution for one of its drilling clients. To handle the huge amount of realtime data, Dynogram used techniques including storage in a central repository and edge processing at the collection point. The goal was to compare realtime data with historical failure rate models. The result was a decrease in repair costs because problems were detected early enough to allow quicker, cheaper repairs.

This model is a reminder that the IoT's emphasis on realtime data doesn't mean there isn't also a role for historical data. It remains important to provide perspective, and further complicates the challenge, because data analytics must also make it possible to contrast the realtime data with historical patterns.

Rockwell is a major supplier to oil drilling components. Its clients include a Hilcorp Energy platform off the Kenai Peninsula in Alaska, which, as is typical in the industry, runs around the clock. Hilcorp worried about potential revenue losses of up to $300,000 daily if a single pump failed, even with the new highly efficient and reliable electrical submersible pumps it installed, which included Rockwell variable speed drives.

Rockwell fed data from the drives to the Microsoft Azure cloud, allowing constant monitoring from the company offices in Cleveland using digital dashboards displaying pressure, temperature, flow rates, and other performance indicators. Critical to predictive maintenance, the Rockwell engineers are notified immediately of any impending problem.

Because of the industrywide drops in productivity, McKinsey benchmarked performance of North Sea platforms, and found that the best performers didn't have excessive costs, in large part because predictive maintenance reduced their unexpected losses and excessive repair costs. The increased production efficiency mentioned previously translated into $220 million to $260 million increased bottom-line results on a single brownfield asset and can extend field life for older wells—not to mention new ones, where the oil company can design in the new monitoring equipment for less than if they had to add it later.[40]

The McKinsey study has implications for all IoT strategies, because they stressed they were interested not just in data quantity but also its quality and how it is used in oil rig decision making:

> Some companies struggle to maintain data quality across their IT networks. Others are not good enough at aggregating data and conducting meaningful analyses. Yet others experience challenges in turning analysis into action. That's why many oil and gas operators need to identify the information shortfalls or leakages that occur when capturing data from processes, systems, and data stores and move them to where operational and business decisions are made. Having identified the leakages, they must then address them by improving the automation of their data flows.[41]

While beyond the scope of this book, a careful reading of the McKinsey report would help anyone designing a predictive maintenance strategy. The McKinsey team outlined three commonsense steps any team designing a data-based predictive maintenance strategy should take:

1. Use multidisciplinary teams (this will be addressed in the next chapter and is crucial to achieve the full benefit of any IoT initiative because they, by nature, involve so many functions).
2. Distinguish between greenfield and brownfield automation, because the greenfield ones have an immediate advantage since sensors and data analytics can be designed in from the beginning, rather than added later.
3. "Thinking big, piloting small, scaling fast," considering total lifecycle costs. "They build a digitization team and make automation part of a corporate digitization program. Their automation programs are integrated with all aspects of their complex organizations, work processes, and human behaviors. Industry experience and prudent risk management dictate that this level of complexity be thoroughly tested and proved in small-scale pilot implementations. Once the concept is proved, rapid scaling is needed to secure the payoff. Such a scale-up requires tools and capabilities in technology-enabled transformation, change, and risk management."[42]

The last is important for all IoT strategy projects. Throughout, an effective IoT strategy must be expansive and holistic.

SUBSTITUTING SERVICES FOR PRODUCTS

Finally, as we try to sequentially map out what can't be mapped sequentially because it is inherently a circular process, we come to the possibility of using the IoT to substitute marketing comprehensive services instead of selling products.

Substituting services for the sale of products must come last in the transition to full IoT implementation. Until your products have been redesigned to build in realtime feedback from the field, you have created communications channels directly between your company and customers, and quality is increased dramatically through predictive maintenance so the product is reliable and ready to serve customers almost all the time, it would be economic folly to consider it.

Once again turning to a product where quality and dependability is a matter of literal life-and-death as the source of strategic direction, we look again at jet turbines, mentioned in the chapter about Siemens and GE. GE and its main competitors are all making the shift to marketing their jet turbines as services instead of just selling them.

The jet turbine business is quite likely the most advanced of *any* industry in incorporating the IoT in terms of amount of data analyzed and earliest implementation of designed-in sensors—not to mention having the highest stakes for failure. This makes it the best place for companies such as yours to look for a detailed road map of how the IoT will evolve in the near future as more operations are monitored, the data volume explodes, and new analytical tools are created. These companies also provide a microcosm of the future of the IoT because the data streams their engines create must also interface with a bewildering array of other systems that must be mashed up, from the airlines' own systems to the FAA. This will inevitably happen in your business when new synergies are found between previously isolated data streams. For example, they are leading the way on collaboration with others within the aviation industry to increase the overall amount of in-flight data and its realtime analysis and application.

Of most interest to us in this aspect of the IoT transformation, these companies have also leveraged this leadership in data gathering and analysis into a fundamental transformation of what they do and how they profit from it: a true paradigm shift in their business models.

Think about how gutsy that is, and at the same time, how the turbine manufacturers really had no choice but to become IoT pioneers. Needless to say, passengers on a plane whose engine(s) fail in midflight will have white knuckles until it (hopefully) lands safely. Beyond those life-or-death issues, airlines are distressed if they face high emergency repair bills and flight delays due to a failure. As a result, anything the turbine manufacturers can do to reduce risk is a necessity. Does your company have a similar pain point?

GE is rising to the challenge through a combination of factors impossible before the IoT:

- Improved design because realtime feedback in flight identifies parts that should be upgraded
- Improved performance by their clients' planes because some airlines choose to pay extra for access to realtime flight data that they can mash up with facts such as fuel prices and atmospheric conditions

- Speedy repairs because they get immediate warnings about impending problems such as metal fatigue or fluid wear so that ground crews can be ready with necessary parts when the plane lands
- More precise manufacturing
- Contributing to the airlines' overall performance when the turbine data is combined with data from other sensors, such as on the wings, and from a growing variety of other realtime streams such as weather and air traffic

The turbine manufacturers have used limited data from the engines for a while, but the volume and speed picked up around 2010 through a combination of faster communications devices and improved wireless sensors.

Faced with the same issues as other companies of still having to deal with a stock of existing, less sophisticated older engines as well as the state-of-the-art ones with IoT sensors built in, GE signed a deal with Avionica that will bring realtime data transfer to the CF34-3 engines. According to former GE general manager Tom Hoferer, previously "the only way to get the diagnostic data we need [was] to stick a flash drive into the engine data computer and download a nasty text file and send it to a computer and email it to an inbox at GE. We really see this as an opportunity to bring some digital life into an older aircraft and use some of that continuous engine operation data."[43]

Just as your companies will expand their data horizons as new technology becomes available, new sensors (and installing more of them) lets these companies also track factors such as temperature, pressure, various rotor speeds, and vibration. In fact, the numbers of sensors being installed in the turbines is astonishing. In Pratt and Whitney's case, they now install five thousand sensors on the Geared Turbo Fan engine, generating up to 10 GB of data *per second*, or up to 844 TB of data on an average twelve-hour flight. That translates into three times as many reports from each engine. Lynn Fraga, Pratt & Whitney's manager of business analytics and engine services, says the company "is currently exploring IoT concepts that will help improve its engine connectivity diagnostics and prognostics capabilities. She believes the next generation of engine health monitoring will stem from the use of more enhanced flight data acquisition storage and transmission technologies."[44] When you combine all the data streams from all the jet turbines, there are predictions that the total data volume could surpass the consumer internet.[45]

Again, the turbine industry serves as a precursor for the IoT transformation of industry in general as it assimilates emerging technologies and seamlessly feeds that data into all aspects of its operations. In this case, that means adding Artificial Intelligence. Because of the huge volumes of data the GTF engines give off, Pratt & Whitney can now build AI to predict the engines' demands and in turn adjust thrust levels. This reduces fuel consumption by 10 to 15 percent, while reducing engine noise and emissions. Similarly, GE's newest engines can yield 5 to 10 TB of data daily, and applying this data to its aviation "Brilliant Factory," the company thinks manufacturing efficiency will increase up to an astonishing 40 percent.[46] Another company is using the data in the design process to simulate performance under various conditions, deploying data analytics in manufacturing for each component, and then, once they are in the air, monitoring the parts' performance selling them as a service.

Once again, the companies' experience demonstrates that you must ask "who else can use this data?" and share it continuously throughout your company and with your customers.

All of these statistics may cause your eyes to glaze over, but they are indicative of what will become commonplace as the IoT is deployed in other industries in the near future. These volumes of data will allow insights, and with them, new services and profit models that were previously inconceivable. How might similar data explosions transform your industry and company?

"POWER BY THE HOUR"

Most important, all of this realtime data and the improved performance and reduced unplanned maintenance that it will allow creates the context for the last element in the IoT transformation that we will discuss. Because devices are so much more valuable and because we now can mash up the engine performance data with other data streams such as weather or data from the planes' fuselages, turbine manufacturers have been able to reduce their reliance on sales and instead create variations on the "power by the hour" leasing concept, where the airlines only pay for the turbines when they are actually generating power—not when they are sitting on the ground or being repaired.

There's a final lesson for companies from the jet turbine makers' experience: Don't assume that you can get complacent because you are increasing reliability and helping customers operate more efficiently. Customer expectations have ratcheted up, and companies must constantly figure out ways to meld new data sources from others into what they provide customers.

There can be no question, given the range of companies that wholeheartedly embrace the IoT and pursue integrated strategies that simultaneously change how they manufacture, design, market, and service things by fully merging the digital and physical, that the IoT is now mature enough that other companies may safely follow their lead. Looking back, it is understandable that these particular companies and industries would have taken the lead, largely because of the extreme circumstances they faced.

However, their leadership in embracing the IoT now reduces the risk for those following in their footsteps. The benefits for both early- and latecomers will dramatically increase because of the network effect phenomenon: the more products and services are IoT-based and the more the resulting data is shared resulting in synergies between them, the more that *all* will become robust and multifaceted.

At the same time, as the final chapter will demonstrate, there is even more mutual benefit that can result from embracing the IoT. Would you believe that it could also spark the first fundamental shift in corporate processes and organization since the birth of the Industrial Age?

SELF-ASSESSMENT

1. Have you begun to think of a synergistic IoT strategy that would target not just product design, manufacturing, marketing, or maintenance, but all of these areas simultaneously, because of how the changes in one area would simultaneously affect the others and increase the benefits?

2. Do you see how fully capitalizing on the IoT will require an integrated strategy that addresses all of these issues simultaneously, rather than selectively dealing only with one or a few of them?

3. What are you doing to bring realtime data to your workers on the factory floor?

4. Have you altered your design process to incorporate the design thinking philosophy?

5. Would a switch from selling products to services be appropriate to your products? What would the necessary first steps be in terms of improving product reliability? What would the benefits be to you and your customers?

8

The Circular Company

W e have seen how the IoT can change how we design, manufacture, market, and maintain a staggering variety of things, inextricably melding the physical and digital worlds. Doesn't it make sense that such sweeping change might also affect how we structure and run the companies that make these things?

In their second article about the IoT in the *Harvard Business Review*, PTC CEO James Heppelmann and Harvard professor Michael Porter raised this issue without answering it:

> For companies grappling with the transition [to the IoT], organizational issues are now center stage—and there is no playbook. We are just beginning the process of rewriting the organization chart that has been in place for decades.[1]

Once they have applied IoT technologies and internalized the Essential Truths attitudinal changes described in Chapter 3, many companies may find themselves ready for the most rev-olutionary change the IoT makes possible, answering the issue raised by Heppelmann and Porter.

That is to abandon obsolete, traditional hierarchies and linear processes for a new Circular Company style suited to today's challenges and technology, especially the newfound ability to "see" inside things. In this new paradigm, information silos and boundaries will be replaced by a new reality in which everyone who needs access to realtime data in order to do their jobs more efficiently and to make better decisions will be able to share that information in realtime.

To fully capitalize on such a shift, we must fundamentally change not just our products, but also the companies that make them. The old model, of hierarchy and linear processes, is no longer relevant to the new reality of being able to see every-thing about things.

It is time to switch to the Circular Company, with realtime data as the hub around which every internal function as well as the supply chain, distribution network, and customers contin-uously revolve.

The benefits of such a shift include:

- Even more precision and efficiency than would already be possible with the IoT
- Streamlining of processes because things that are now done sequentially could be done simultaneously
- Unprecedented creativity from bringing many perspec-tives, skill sets, and even personal experiences to bear on the same challenges simultaneously

This vision of circular organizations is speculative. To my knowledge, no one else writing about the IoT has suggested it. Yet I believe it is a logical consequence of the IoT.

The change to Circular Companies would be a wrenching, dramatic shift from business as usual. To my knowledge, there is neither a specific example of it in practice or a road map to the transformation. However, the new realities and tools are in place that would make it possible—at least hypothetically—so I offer it in hopes that management thinkers and a few brave managers will take the challenge and make it a reality. As with scientific revolutions, just because there's no precedent doesn't mean it can't or shouldn't be tried.

When the Industrial Revolution began, there were two models for large organizations, the Catholic Church and the army, and, because of the lack of realtime data on things, it made sense for these new companies to manage information the way those organizations did: top down, and in linear fashion, parceled out to different departments sequentially and when senior management decided it was relevant. In fact, the early railroads often turned directly to the army for policies and procedures.[2]

Today, as we've seen in so many cases in this book, the limits on data gathering and sharing have been removed. In addition, collaborative tools such as Slack and workstyles such as Scrum have become robust and increasingly popular. Yet even IoT startups are still structured on the old hierarchical and linear models.

Even though hierarchies were the understandable organizational form for the early Industrial Age, circular ones predate it. Think of our fur-clad ancestors circling around a campfire to plot how to kill the saber-toothed tiger, or King Arthur, who didn't line his knights up but gathered them around the round table. And don't forget nature, which has done pretty well for 4.54 billion years operating on a cyclical basis.

Think visually for a moment.

Circles are inherently collaborative. Everyone can see and talk to each other. There is no obvious sign of supremacy or rank. When it comes to exercising decisions, the circle inherently closes the loop so that data and other information come back to the beginning, rather than petering off in a linear and dead-end process. No wonder companies back in the 1980s formed quality circles to improve performance. They didn't call for quality squares, did they?

There's an analogy between the possibility of a shift from hierarchical to circular management and similar radical shifts in science, as explained by Thomas Kuhn in his landmark *The Structure of Scientific Revolutions*.[3] Kuhn wrote of how there's a typical pattern when an old paradigm (such as the Ptolemeian view of the universe) is about to collapse. More and more anomalies occur that can't be explained by the old "truth," until we reach a crisis and a new paradigm quickly emerges:

> Crisis simultaneously loosens the stereotypes and provides the incremental data necessary for a fundamental paradigm shift. Sometimes the shape of the new paradigm is foreshadowed in the structure that extraordinary research has given to the anomaly. . . . More often no such structure is consciously seen in advance. Instead, the new paradigm, or a sufficient hint to permit later articulation, emerges all at once,

sometimes in the middle of the night, in the mind of a man deeply immersed in crisis. What the nature of that final stage is—how an individual invents (or finds he has invented) a new way of giving order to data now all assembled—must here remain inscrutable and may be permanently so. Let us here note only one thing about it. Almost always the men who achieve these fundamental inventions of a new paradigm have been either very young or very new to the field whose paradigm they change. . . . And perhaps that point need not have been made explicit, for obviously these are the men who, being little committed by prior practice to the traditional rules of normal science, are particularly likely to see that those rules no longer define a playable game and to conceive another set that can replace them.[4]

Could the increasing number of instances where work groups have chosen collaboration and innovators have created collaboration tools be the anomalies that trigger such a management paradigm shift? Could it be millennials, "very young or very new to the field," whose well-known aversion to hierarchy and love of collaboration drives the change?

LOOK TO W. L. GORE FOR INSPIRATION

How might such a system be organized and function, especially if its premise is that more than two hundred years of pretty successful business practices must be changed?

Perhaps the closest approximation of the Circular Company to be found in existing businesses is W. L. Gore & Associates, a consistent innovator. Since its formation in 1958, the company has been organized on a "lattice" model (i.e., every worker is connected to every other worker), based on founder Bill Gore's experiences with freeform task forces for special projects when he worked at DuPont. [5] There are "no traditional organizational charts, no chains of command, nor predetermined channels of communication." Instead, they use cross-disciplinary teams including all functions, communicating directly with each other.

Teams self-organize at Gore, and most leaders emerge rather than being anointed: They call it "natural leadership." One individual may actually take on what would be several different jobs at traditional companies, such as sales and product design. The company also thinks small size is important to allowing everyone to be a participant and be heard, so new facilities are built nearby when an existing one gets to about two hundred employees. [6]

As Deloitte's Cathy Benko and Molly Anderson wrote, "Continuing to invest in the future using yesteryear's industrial blueprint is futile. The lattice redefines workplace suppositions, providing a framework for organizing and advancing a company's existing incremental efforts into a comprehensive, strategic response to the changing world of work." [7]

Others, most notably Russell Ackoff in the 1990s, have proposed circular organizational styles in the past, but they have never taken off. [8] My argument is that what makes today different in terms of the potential for circular organizations is that, for the first time, the realtime data from every aspect of the organization (and, for these purposes, that also includes the supply chain, distribution network, retailers, and customers using the products every day in the field) can be gathered and shared instantly.

As we have seen, that changes everything.

In the past, it was equally hard to gather the data and to share it, so it made sense for management to parcel out things as it saw fit.

Contrast that to realtime sharing of realtime data.

If you can share data instantly, does it still make sense to deal with it sequentially?

Think about it.

Restating what we have discussed and what innovators are already profiting from, that data coming in right now from the operating product can be used at the same time (with the digital twin as the frame of reference) by:

- **Maintenance,** to predict possible problems and intervene via predictive maintenance to minimize the cost and interruption the customer needs

- **Design,** to document patterns of problems either with parts or ease of use that can be used to design upgrades that will be more dependable and user friendly

- **Marketing,** to see if there are consistent patterns of product misuse that indicate the need to rewrite the manual, or to add new features

- **Supply chain partners,** to see if certain parts need to be replaced more frequently in one area than another (for example, jet turbine parts in areas with windblown sand)

Even more important is the potential for innovation and creativity if all those groups look at and can discuss the data—ground truth—simultaneously. That's where new group-ware and sharing technologies comes in.

Take Scrum, for instance. Originally created for software design projects, it is now being used for all types of complex and interactive projects. It emphasizes rapid development, primarily by "chunking" the overall project, and then the group creates a "sprint" deadline of several weeks to complete the work, meeting daily to discuss the progress—"daily Scrum." After the sprint, that chunk should be ready to hand to the customer. After a sprint review, the team chooses another chunk and works on it.

Why not make a similar approach to management continuous? That doesn't mean every team member would have to weigh in constantly. Contributions could be made asynchronously, archived so that others could comment later.

Similarly, Slack and other groupware enable much simpler collaboration than is possible with email, especially with its primary reliance on channels, which are like chatrooms. Because they aren't limited to private communication but can be shared, they facilitate brainstorming and collaboration.[9]

Clearly, the growing popularity of these programs and work-styles shows the underlying demand for collaboration and circular approaches. Indeed, "a Work.com study found that 97 percent of employees and executives agreed that the level of collaboration directly impacts the outcome of a task or project."[10]

Think of how many steps in the various interrelated phases of the IoT could work with such an institutional framework.

- The digital twin could be the consistent focus for all functional groups, so they would always be focused on the smart, connected product. The cyclical design process that has shaved off so much time for GE could become the norm.

- Supply chain partners who could see the current status of production could resupply in time to avoid interruptions. More likely, this would be done automatically, through M2M processes.

- Realtime sales and distribution data could alert the assembly line to slow or increase production.

- Predictive maintenance data would help designers target parts and assemblies where there were consistent problems.

The results could be dramatic. In a survey by WiPro Digital and Forum for the Future, they found that "focusing on cross-functional discipline can lead to the creation of disruptive and systematic solutions. When employees are networking and actively sharing projects and resources freely across departments, it creates a fluid exchange of information among groups and individuals of varying areas of expertise, which in turn can spark new ideas and inspire experimentation. Innovation often follows."[11]

Yes, there would be thorny questions to answer to make such a system work. There still would be a need for a formal reporting structure to avoid chaos (W. L. Gore has a limited number of leaders with official titles). Supply chain and distribution network partners would only get limited information, on a need-to-know basis, and this could only be done with those partners with which you had built long-term, trusted relationships. Assembly line workers using software such as Tulip would only get the information relevant to their work.

Many managers would also have to change their attitudes, according to a recent Harvard Business Review Services survey, which found that for any company that wants to be more collaborative:

First, the culture must allow decisionmaking input from the workforce, with a flatter, more open organizational structure. Second, a collaborative organization must promote interaction among departments, enabled by state-of-the art communication and document sharing and remote access to information and each other.[12]

There would also be significant attitudinal obstacles. The same survey found that the biggest obstacle to collaboration was lack of management support, and that real management participation was ranked higher than simple management support for collaboration.[13]

It may well be that there are insuperable obstacles to the Circular Company vision that make such a shift impossible, such as how to protect corporate secrets or how to enforce accountability. Or maybe, despite their problems and shortcomings, hierarchy and linear processes are good enough.

On the other hand, hierarchy and linear processes were necessary coping mechanisms to deal with the Collective Blindness that afflicted us all in the past, but the IoT removes that obstacle. If nature is cyclical and the earliest forms of human organization were cyclical, wouldn't the Circular Company be more natural?

Just think about it.

SELF-ASSESSMENT

1. Has your company encountered problems where traditional hierarchy and linear processes have interfered with solutions? Have you just put up with those obstacles, or tried to remove them?

2. Have you used groupware and teams to deal with especially difficult and challenging problems? If so, why? What were the benefits and results? Why did you reserve those approaches for special issues while retaining hierarchy and linear processes for your overall daily operations?

NOTES

PREFACE

1. W. David Stephenson, *Data Dynamite*, Boston: Data4All Press, 2011.
2. W. David Stephenson, *Managing the Internet of Things Revolution*. SAP: 2014. http://theiotrevolution.com/iguide/
3. W. David Stephenson, "The Buckyball Corporation." *Network World*, April 1995.

INTRODUCTION

1. Michael Porter and James Heppelmann, "How Smart, Connected Products are Transforming Companies," *Harvard Business Review*, October 2015, p. 19. https://hbr.org/2015/10/how-smart-connected-products-are-transforming-companies

CHAPTER 1

1. John B. Kennedy, "When Woman Is Boss," *Colliers*, January 30, 1926. http://www.tfcbooks.com/tesla/1926-01-30.htm
2. BigBelly Solar Marketing VP Leila Dillon, telephone interview, October 20, 2017.
3. Author's note: I am a purist about language and usage, but I've thrown in the towel when it comes to data, which, classically, is plural. (The singular is datum.) However, data as a singular noun is so common now that it is becoming accepted and actually (to me) sounds better, so that will be the usage in this book.
4. "Clinical Research From HRS Validates AliveCor Delivers Value-Based Care for Heart Health," *AliveCor* (news release), May 12, 2016. https://www.alivecor.com/en/press/press_release/clinical-research-from-hr-validates/

5. "The Rise of Mobile: 11.6 Billion Mobile-Connected Devices By 2020," *Mobile Future*, February 4, 2016. http://mobile future.org/the-rise-of-mobile-11-6-billion-mobile-connected-devices-by-2020/

6. Joseph Bradley, Jeff Loucks, James Macaulay, and Andy Noronha, "Internet of Everything (IoE) Value Index: How Much Value Are Private-Sector Firms Capturing from IoE in 2013?" *Cisco*, 2013. https://www.cisco.com/c/dam/en_us/about/ac79/docs/innov/IoE-Value_Index_White-Paper.pdf

7. "The Internet of Things: Consumer, Industrial & Public Services 2016–2021," *Juniper Research*, December 14, 2016. https://www.juniperresearch.com/researchstore/iot-m2m/internet-of-things/consumer-industrial-public-services

8. "Internet of Things (IoT) Market: Global Demand, Growth Analysis & Opportunity Outlook 2023," *Research Nester*, October 3, 2017. https://www.researchnester.com/reports/internet-of-things-iot-market-global-demand-growth-analysis-opportunity-outlook-2023/216

9. Peter Evans and Marco Annunziata, "Industrial Internet: Pushing the Boundaries of Minds and Machines," *General Electric*, 2012. http://www.geautomation.com/download/industrial-internet-pushing-boundaries-minds-and-machines

10. Gil Press, "It's Official: The Internet of Things Takes Over Big Data as the Most Hyped Technology," *Forbes*, August 18, 2014. https://www.forbes.com/sites/gilpress/2014/08/18/its-official-the-internet-of-things-takes-over-big-data-as-the-most-hyped-technology/

11. The Economist Intelligence Unit, "The Internet of Things Business Index: A Quiet Revolution Gathers Pace," *Economist*, 2013. https://www.arm.com/files/pdf/EIU_Internet_Business_Index_WEB.PDF

12. Jeffrey Conklin, *Dialogue Mapping: Building Shared Understanding of Wicked Problems*, p. x. Wiley, 2006.

13. "Improve Efficiency and Work Smarter by Lighting up Dark Assets," *Connected Futures,* March, 2015. http://www.connectedfuturesmag.com/a/S15A9/improve-efficiency-and-work-smarter-by-lighting-up-dark-assets/?utm_source=tw&utm_medium=twt&utm_campaign=gr_242015_c#.WfiPGltKsWo

14. Erik Brynjolfsson and Andrew McAfee, *The Second Machine Age: Work, Progress and Prosperity in a Time of Brilliant Technologies*, New York: Norton, 2014, p. 79.

15. Kennedy, *op.cit.*

16. IEEE Internet of Things, "Towards a definition of the Internet of Things (IoT)," *IEEE*, May 13, 2015. http://iot.ieee.org/ images/files/pdf/IEEE_IoT_Towards_Definition_Internet_of_ Things_Issue1_14MAY15.pdf

17. Fredrick Gunnarsson, Johan Williamson, Jerome Buvat, Roopa Nambiar, Ashish Bisht, "The Internet of Things: Are Organizations Ready for a Multi-Trillion Dollar Prize?" Cap Gemini Digital Transformation Research Institute, 2015.

CHAPTER 2

1. Andy Greenberg, "Hackers Remotely Kill a Jeep on the Highway—With Me in It," *Wired*, July 2015. https://www.wired .com/2015/07/hackers-remotely-kill-jeep-highway/

2. Kasmir Hill, "How A Creep Hacked a Baby Monitor to Say Lewd Things to a 2-Year-Old," *Forbes*, August 13, 2013. https://www.forbes.com/sites/kashmirhill/2013/08/13/how- a-creep-hacked-a-baby-monitor-to-say-lewd-things-to-a-2-year- old/#79bbca43aad6

3. Darrell Ethrington and Kate Conger, "Large DDoS attacks cause outages at Twitter, Spotify, and other sites," *TechCrunch*, October 21, 2016. https://techcrunch.com/2016/10/21/ many-sites-including-twitter-and-spotify-suffering-outage/

4. Dan Goldman, "Shodan: the Scariest Search Engine on the Internet," *CNN*, April 8, 2013. http://money.cnn .com/2013/04/08/technology/security/shodan/index.html

5. J. M. Porup, "'Internet of Things' Security Is Hilariously Broken and Getting Worse," *Ars Technica*, January 23, 2016. https://arstechnica.com/information-technology/2016/01/ how-to-search-the-internet-of-things-for-photos-of-sleeping- babies/

6. European Union Agency for Network and Information Security, *Privacy and Data Protection by Design—from Police to Engineering*, December 2014. https://www.enisa.europa.eu/ publications/privacy-and-data-protection-by-design

7. Edith Ramirez, "Privacy By Design and the New Privacy Framework of the U.S. Federal Trade Commission," Federal Trade Commission: June 13, 2012. https://www.ftc.gov/sites/default/files/documents/public_statements/privacy-design-and-new-privacy-framework-u.s.federal-trade-commission/120613privacydesign.pdf; "Strategic Principles for Securing the Internet of Things (IoT)," U.S. Department of Homeland Security, November 2016. https://www.dhs.gov/sites/default/files/publications/Strategic_Principles_for_Securing_the_Internet_of_Things-2016-1115-FINAL_v2-dg11.pdf

8. European Union Agency for Network and Information Security, *op.cit.*

9. Ibid., p. 6.

10. Ibid., p. 117.

11. *IoT Security Foundation*. https://www.iotsecurityfoundation.org/; *BuildItSecure.ly* https://builditsecure.ly/#goals

12. "Internet of Things: Privacy & Security in a Connected World," Federal Trade Commission, November 2013. https://www.ftc.gov/system/files/documents/reports/federal-trade-commission-staff-report-november-2013-workshop-entitled-internet-things-privacy/150127iotrpt.pdf

13. Bhoopathi Rapolu, "Internet Of Aircraft Things: An Industry Set To Be Transformed," *Aviation Week*, January 18, 2016. http://aviationweek.com/connected-aerospace/internet-aircraft-things-industry-set-be-transformed

14. Heather Clancy, "How GE Generates $1 Billion From Data," *Fortune*, October 10, 2014. http://fortune.com/2014/10/10/ge-data-robotics-sensors/

15. Author's note: SAP is a client of mine.

16. Elvia Wallis, "Quench Your Thirst for Innovation with Smart Vending Machines," *SAP Blogs*, July 28, 2016. https://blogs.sap.com/2016/07/28/quench-your-thirst-for-innovation-with-smart-vending-machines/

17. "Waiting to Exhale: GPS Inhalers Identify Asthma Hotspots," *Propeller Health*, November 26, 2012. https://www.propellerhealth.com/2012/11/26/governing-waiting-to-exhale-gps-inhalers-identify-asthma-hotspots/

18. Nick Stockton, "Boston is Partnering with Waze to Make Its Roads Less of a Nightmare," *Wired*, February 20, 2015.

https://www.wired.com/2015/02/boston-partnering-waze-make-roads-less-nightmare/

19. Katie Jackson, "Columbus Under Construction to Become America's First 'Smart City,'" *Fox News*, July 10, 2016. http://www.foxnews.com/tech/2017/07/10/columbus-under-construction-to-become-americas-first-smart-city.html

20. LoRaWAN doesn't need 3G or Wi-Fi to connect with the internet. There are no Wi-Fi passwords, mobile subscriptions have no setup costs, and the system features low battery usage, long range, and low bandwidth.

21. W. David Stephenson, "Data is the Hub: How the IoT and Circular Economy Build Profits," *Stephenson Blogs on the Internet of Things* (blog), November 2, 2015. http://www.stephensonstrategies.com/data-is-the-hub-how-the-iot-and-circular-economy-build-profits/

22. Incidentally, the Durathon and Grundfos examples illustrate a good strategy to look for creative IoT solutions: devices that are extremely expensive to make and repair, which are located in hard-to-reach locations. From Formula One race cars to offshore oil rigs, the IoT is already in full use.

23. Quentin Hardy, "G.E.'s 'Industrial Internet' Goes Big," *New York Times*, October 9, 2013. https://bits.blogs.nytimes.com/2013/10/09/g-e-s-industrial-internet-goes-big/?_r=1

24. SC Digest Editorial Staff, "Physical Twins Provide Data Over Time That Allows Digital Version to Simulate and Optimize Performance, Among Other Benefits," *Supply Chain Digest*, August 30, 2017. http://www.scdigest.com/ontarget/17-08-30-1.php?cid=12930

25. Zvi Feuer, "Smart Factory—The Factory of the Future," *Siemens PLM Community*, December 16, 2016. https://community.plm.automation.siemens.com/t5/Digital-Transformations/Smart-Factory-The-Factory-of-the-Future/ba-p/381717

26. W. David Stephenson, "Why the Internet of Things Will Bring Fundamental Change: What Can You Do Now That You Couldn't Do Before?," *Stephenson Blogs on Internet of Things* (blog), August 12, 2014. http://www.stephensonstrategies.com/why-the-internet-of-things-will-bring-fundamental-change-what-can-you-do-now-that-you-couldnt-do-before/

27. Alex Brisbourne, "Tesla's Over-the-Air Fix: Best Example Yet of the Internet of Things?" *Wired,* February 2014. https://www.wired.com/insights/2014/02/teslas-air-fix-best-example-yet-internet-things/

CHAPTER 3

1. The *Postscapes* website, perhaps the best overall IoT reference source, has an exhaustive IoT history. https://www.postscapes.com/internet-of-things-history/
2. Mark Weiser, "The Computer for the 21st Century," *Scientific American*, September, 1991. http://www.ubiq.com/hypertext/weiser/SciAmDraft3.html
3. Ibid.
4. Gil Press, "A Very Short History of the Internet of Things," *Forbes*, June 14, 2014. https://www.infosys.com/insights/services-being-digital/Documents/future-industrial-digital.pdf
5. Ibid.
6. Travis Andrews, "Robotics Are Helping Paralyzed People Walk Again, but the Price Tag Is Huge," *Washington Post*, June 12, 2017. https://www.washingtonpost.com/news/morning-mix/wp/2017/06/10/robotics-are-helping-paralyzed-people-walk-again-but-the-price-tag-is-huge/?utm_term=.12f1cd671cce
7. John Kennedy, "The Machines Are Coming: How M2M Spawned the Internet of Things," *Silicon Republic*, May 18, 2016. https://www.siliconrepublic.com/machines/m2m-cutting-edge-machines-internet-of-things-explained
8. Press, *op.cit.*
9. Ingrid Lunden, "6.1B Smartphone Users Globally By 2020, Overtaking Basic Fixed Phone Subscriptions," *TechCrunch*, June 2, 2015. https://techcrunch.com/2015/06/02/6-1b-smartphone-users-globally-by-2020-overtaking-basic-fixed-phone-subscriptions/
10. Email from Prescott Logan, former general manager, GE Energy Storage. March 8, 2018.
11. Thor Olavsrud, "10 Principles of a Successful IoT Strategy," *CIO*, January 30, 2017. https://www.cio.com/article/3162995/internet-of-things/10-principles-of-a-successful-iot-strategy.html

12. "VNI Global Fixed and Mobile Internet Traffic Forecasts," *Cisco*. https://www.cisco.com/c/en/us/solutions/service-provider/visual-networking-index-vni/index.html

13. Matthew Perry, "Evaluating and Choosing an IoT Platform," O'Reilly Media, 2016. https://www.ptc.com/en/resources/iot/white-paper/choosing-iot-platform

14. "AI Commentator," *AGT*, last modified March 7, 2018. https://www.agtinternational.com/software-platforms/ai-commentator/

15. Rita L. Sallam, W. Roy Schulte, Gerald Van Hoy, Jim Hare, "Cool Vendors in Internet of Things Analytics," Gartner: May 11, 2016.

16. "SlantRange: powerful new information for agriculture." www.slantrange.com

17. Joe Biron and Jonathan Follett, *Foundational Elements of an IoT Solution*, O'Reilly Media, 2016, p. 47.

18. Wyatt Carlson, "10 IoT Platforms Changing How Companies Do Business," SDxCentral, May 29, 2017. https://www.sdxcentral.com/articles/news/10-iot-platforms-changing-how-companies-do-business/2017/05/

19. "Researchers Use 3D-Printer to Make Tiny Batteries," *The Daily Fusion*, June 24, 2013. http://dailyfusion.net/2013/06/researchers-use-3d-printer-to-make-tiny-batteries-11947/

20. Allied Market Research, "Global Sensor Market Forecast 2022: IoT and Wearables as Drivers," *I-Scoop*. https://www.i-scoop.eu/global-sensor-market-forecast-2022/

21. W. David Stephenson, "Sound's Emerging IoT role," *Stephenson Blogs on the Internet of Things*, March 7, 2017. http://www.stephensonstrategies.com/sounds-emerging-iot-role/

22. IoT Marketplace. https://www.the-iot-marketplace.com/

23. Libelium CEO Alicia Asín, phone interview with author, December 21, 2017.

24. Anura P. Jayasumana, Qi Han, and Tissa H. Illangasekare, "Virtual Sensor Networks: A Resource Efficient Approach for Concurrent Applications," Dept. of Electrical & Computer Engineering, Colorado State University, November 12, 2012. http://www.cnrl.colostate.edu/Projects/VSNs/vsns.html

25. Kaivan Karimi, "The Role of Sensor Fusion in the Internet of Things," *Mouser Electronics*. https://ca.mouser.com/applications/sensor-fusion-iot/

26. W. David Stephenson, "IoT and AI: Made for Each Other," *PTC Product Lifecycle Report*, 2017. https://www.ptc.com/en/product-lifecycle-report/iot-and-ai-made-for-each-other

27. Ibid.

28. Zoe Gross, "The Dark Side of the Coin: Bitcoin and Crime," *Finfeed*, Sep 5, 2017. https://finfeed.com/features/dark-side-coin-bitcoin-crime/20170905/; Nolan Bauerle, "What Are the Applications and Uses of Blockchain?" *Coindesk*. https://www.coindesk.com/information/applications-use-cases-blockchains/

29. W. David Stephenson, "Blockchain Might Be the Answer to IoT Security Woes," *Stephenson Blogs on Internet of Things*, December 19, 2016. http://www.stephensonstrategies.com/blockchain-might-be-answer-to-iot-security-woes/

30. Ibid.

CHAPTER 4

1. Saju Skaria, "Digital Twins," *Saju Skaria: Random Thoughts on Leadership, Strategies, Global Business, and Spirituality.* December 28, 2016. http://sajuskaria.blogspot.com/2016/12/digital-twins.html

2. Daniel Newman, "Digital Twins: The Business Imperative You Might Not Know About," *Forbes*, May 30, 2017. https://www.forbes.com/sites/danielnewman/2017/05/30/digital-twins-the-business-imperative-you-might-not-know-about/#3a041e89693c

3. "Millions of Things Will Soon Have Digital Twins," *The Economist*, July 13, 2017. https://www.economist.com/news/business/21725033-factories-cars-range-consumer-products-millions-things-will-soon-have-digital

4. Dr. Michael Grieves, phone interview with author, December 18, 2017.

5. Ibid.

6. Hardy, *op.cit.*

7. "Millions of things will soon have digital twins," *The Economist*, July 13, 2017.

8. PTC, "Unlocking a World of Possibilities for AR and the IoT," May 19, 2016. https://www.youtube.com/watch?v=155ZO4uWiYc

9. Mark Egan, "'Digital Twin' Technology Changed Formula 1 and Online Ads. Planes, Trains and Power Are Next," GE: October 4, 2015. https://www.ge.com/reports/digital-twin-tech-nology-changed-formula-1-online-ads-planes-trains-power-next/

10. Ariel Schartz, "Singapore Will Soon Have a 'Virtual Twin City' That Reflects Everything in the Real World," *Business Insider*, January 21, 2016. http://www.businessinsider.com/singapore-will-soon-have-a-virtual-twin-city-2016-1

11. Sara Scoles, "A Digital Twin of Your Body Could Become a Critical Part of Your Health Care," *Slate*, February 10, 2016. http://www.slate.com/articles/technology/future_tense/2016/02/dassault_s_living_heart_project_and_the_future_of_digital_twins_in_health.html

12. Kasey Panetta, "Gartner Top 10 Strategic Technology Trends for 2018," *Smarter With Gartner*, October 3, 2017. https://www.gartner.com/smarterwithgartner/gartner-top-10-strategic-technology-trends-for-2018/?utm_source=social&utm_campaign=sm-swg&utm_medium=social Gartner Top 10 StrategicTechnology Trends for 2018; Christy Petty, "Prepare for the Impact of Digital Twins," *Smarter With Gartner*, September 18, 2017. https://www.gartner.com/smarterwithgartner/prepare-for-the-impact-of-digital-twins/

13. Tanja Ruecker, "Making Sense of The New Business Models Powered by Digital Twins." *Manufacturing Business Technology*, October 23, 2017. https://www.mbtmag.com/article/2017/10/making-sense-new-business-models-powered-digital-twins

14. Christie Pettey, "Prepare for the Impact of Digital Twins," *Smarter With Gartner*, September 18, 2017. https://www.gartner.com/smarterwithgartner/prepare-for-the-impact-of-digital-twins/

15. "GE's Digital Wind Farm for Onshore Wind." GE Renewable Energy. https://www.gerenewableenergy.com/wind-energy/technology/digital-wind-farm

16. Bernard Marr, "What is Digital Twin Technology—And Why Is It So Important?," *Forbes*, March 6, 2017. https://www.forbes.com/sites/bernardmarr/2017/03/06/what-is-digital-twin-technology-and-why-is-it-so-important/2/#6c9542d73227

17. Dr. Colin Parris, "Minds + Machines: Meet a Digital Twin," GE Mind + Machines Conference. https://www.youtube.com/ watch?v=2dCz3oL2rTw&t=554s

18. Ibid.

19. "Exelon and GE: Forecasting the Future." https://www .gerenewableenergy.com/stories/exelon-forecasting-future

20. "E.ON and GE: A Power Up Story." https://www.gerenewable energy.com/stories/eon-power-up

21. Erin Biba, "The Jet Engines With Digital Twins," *BBC*, February 14, 2017. http://www.bbc.com/autos/story/20170214-how-jet-engines-are-made

22. CAD Place, "PTC redefines 'Digital Twin' with IoT, Big Data, and Augmented Reality Technology." http://www.cadplace. co.uk/Trends/PTC-redefines-Digital-Twin-with-IoT-big-data-and-augmented-reality-technology

23. W. David Stephenson, "Game-changer! AR Enables IoT merging of physical and digital," *Stephenson Blogs on Internet of Things*, June 21, 2016. http://www.stephensonstrategies.com/ game-changer-ar-enables-iot-merging-of-physical-and-digital/

24. PTC Executive Vice President Michael Campbell, phone interview with the author, January 8, 2018.

25. Parris, *op.cit.*

CHAPTER 5

1. Christoph Wegener and Johannes von Karczewski, *1847–2017—Shaping the Future: Qualities That Set Siemens Apart—After 170 Years*. Siemens, 2017. https://www.siemens.com/ content/dam/webassetpool/mam/tag-siemens-com/smdb/corporate-core/communication-and-gov-affairs/tl/HI/siemens-historical-institute/home/094-shi-siemens-at-170-years-the-siemens-narrative-2017-e.pdf

2. Ibid.

3. Rainer Drath and Alexander Horch, "Industrie 4.0: Hit or Hype?," *IEEE Industrial Electronics Magazine*, June 2014. Industrie 4.0 refers to the 4th industrial revolution, preceded by 1st: mechanization; 2nd: mass production; 3rd: computerization. https://ieeexplore.ieee.org/document/6839101/

4. The Obama administration did fund a $2.2 billion advanced manufacturing initiative in 2013. Christopher Alessi and Chase Gummer, "Germany Bets on 'Smart Factories' to Keep Its Manufacturing Edge," *Wall Street Journal*, October 26, 2014. https://www.wsj.com/articles/germany-bets-on-smart-factories-to-keep-its-manufacturing-edge-1414355745

5. "Defects: A Vanishing Species?" Siemens, October 1, 2014. https://www.siemens.com/innovation/en/home/pictures-of-the-future/industry-and-automation/digital-factories-defects-a-vanishing-species.html

6. Ibid.

7. Susan Cinadr, "PLM on Mars: How NASA JPL Used Siemens Technology to Land Curiosity," Siemens, August 6, 2012.

8. Dr. Sebastian Schoning personal interview, Barcelona, November 2016.

9. W. David Stephenson, "Siemens's Mobility Services: Trains Become IoT Labs on Wheels," *Stephenson Blogs on the Internet of Things*, November 18, 2016. http://www.stephensonstrategies.com/siemenss-mobility-services-trains-become-iot-labs-on-wheels/

10. "Mobility Services Focus on digitalization," Siemens: 2016. http://www.siemens.co.ir/pool/events/mobility-service-brochure.pdf

11. Stephenson, "Siemens's Mobility Services: Trains Become IoT Labs on Wheels," *op.cit.*

12. Ibid.

13. Siemens, *Industry Software—Driving the Digital Enterprise.* https://www.siemens.com/stories/cc/en/driven-by-data/assets/Industry%20Software%20Brochure%202015-ENG.PDF

14. Siemens, *Driven by Data.* https://www.siemens.com/stories/cc/en/driven-by-data/

15. Andrew Hughes, "Siemens and Maserati Show Off Integrated Design and Manufacturing," LNS Research: December 30, 2015. http://blog.lnsresearch.com/siemens-and-maserati-show-off-integrated-design-and-manufacturing

16. Ibid.

17. Jeffrey R. Immelt, "How I Remade GE," *Harvard Business Review*, September–October, 2017. https://hbr.org/2017/09/inside-ges-transformation#how-i-remade-ge

18. Ibid.
19. "GE Digital is taking Predix out to the edge of IoT," *IDG Connect*, November 15, 2016. http://www.idgconnect.com/abstract/22612/ge-digital-taking-predix-edge-iot
20. Marco Annunziata, "The Moment for Industry," GE, October, 2015. https://s3.amazonaws.com/dsg.files.app.content.prod/gereports/wp-content/uploads/2015/09/29153350/Annunziata_Moment-for-industry_Final1.pdf
21. Bill Ruh, "IDC Marketscape Names GE Digital a Leader in IoT Platform Landscape," *GE Digital*, 2017. https://www.ge.com/digital/blog/idc-marketscape-names-ge-digital-leader-iot-platform-software
22. "Brilliant Manufacturing: Digitize to Thrive," GE Digital Manufacturing Solutions. https://www.ge.com/digital/brilliant-manufacturing
23. Dr. Colin Parris, "A Twin-building Army: GE Previews First-ever Digital Twin Analytics Workbench," *GE*, October 24, 2017. https://www.linkedin.com/pulse/twin-building-army-ge-previews-first-ever-digital-twin-colin-parris/
24. Marco Annunziata, "Marco Annunziata: The Industrial App Economy Is Ready for Its Download," *GE Reports*, September 29, 2015. https://www.ge.com/reports/marco-annunziata-the-industrial-app-economy-is-ready-for-its-download/
25. Ranjay Gulati, "GE's Global Growth Experiment," *Harvard Business Review*, September–October 2017. https://hbr.org/2017/09/inside-ges-transformation#ges-global-growth-experiment
26. March 7, 2018, email to author from Prescott Logan, former president and general manager, Energy Storage Unit, GE Power & Water
27. Ron Miller, "In Spite of Digital Transformation, 2017 Did Not Yield the Desired Financial Results for GE," *TechCrunch*, December 10, 2017. https://techcrunch.com/2017/12/10/in-spite-of-digital-transformation-2017-did-not-yield-the-desired-financial-results-for-ge/
28. John Flannery, "Our Future Is Digital," *GE Digital*, October 2017. https://www.ge.com/digital/blog/our-future-digital

CHAPTER 6

1. ABB, "ABB Smart Sensor FAQ." http://new.abb.com/motors-generators/service/advanced-services/smart-sensor/faq

2. IBM Research, "Senet Uses LoRa and IBM Long Range Signaling and Control to Launch New Business Model." https://www.youtube.com/watch?v=OTzBSTROcy8

3. Ken Ying, "How Technology Is Enhancing Shipment Visibility and Saving Lives," *MNX Global Logistics*, March 8, 2017. http://news.mnx.com/2017/03/technology-enhancing-shipment-visibility-saving-lives/

4. Cisco, "Digital Manufacturing Powers a Better Way to Build Trucks." https://www.cisco.com/c/dam/en_us/solutions/industries/docs/manufacturing/daimler-full-customer-case-study.pdf

5. "IoT in Action—Real-World IoT Deployment in an Intel Factory." https://www.intel.com/content/www/us/en/internet-of-things/videos/iot-in-action-video.html

6. "Simpler and Smarter Connections at Germany's Largest Seaport." https://www.sap.com/about/customer-testimonials/public-sector/hamburg-port-authority.html

7. SAP, "Hamburg Port Authority and the Internet of Things." https://www.sap.com/about/customer-testimonials/public-sector/hamburg-port-authority.html#

8. "Pay per Wash: Winterhalter Focuses on Servitization and Becomes the Pioneer of the 'Business Pay-Per-Use' Model in the Food Industry," *Semioty*, November 23, 2017. https://www.semioty.com/en/iot-blog/pay-wash-winterhalter-pioneer-business-model-pay-per-use/

9. Michael Lev-Ram, "What John Deere Is Doing to Fight Slumping Sales," *Fortune*, November 15, 2015. http://fortune.com/2015/11/15/john-deere-software-services-agriculture-data/

10. "The first Smart Vineyard in Lebanon chooses Libelium's technology to face the climate change," Libelium, November 29, 2017. http://www.libelium.com/the-first-smart-vineyard-in-lebanon-chooses-libeliums-technology-to-face-the-climate-change/

11. "Saving Water with Smart Irrigation System in Barcelona," Libelium, August 29, 2016. http://www.libelium.com/saving-water-with-smart-irrigation-system-in-barcelona/

12. Ross Tieman, "Barcelona: Smart City Revolution in Progress," *Financial Times*, October 26, 2017. https://www.ft.com/content/6d2fe2a8-722c-11e7-93ff-99f383b09ff9

13. Stephenson, *Data Dynamite, op.cit.*

14. Ibid.

15. Laura Adler, "How Smart City Barcelona Brought the Internet of Things to Life," *Smart City Solutions*, February 18, 2016. http://datasmart.ash.harvard.edu/news/article/how-smart-city-barcelona-brought-the-internet-of-things-to-life-789

16. Lucas Laursen, "Barcelona's Smart City Ecosystem," *MIT Technology Review*, November 18, 2014. https://www.technologyreview.com/s/532511/barcelonas-smart-city-ecosystem/

17. "New Research Confirms Significance of AliveCor's 30 Second EKG," AliveCor news release, September 6, 2017. https://www.alivecor.com/press/press_release/new-research-confirms-significance-of-alivecors-30-second-ekg/

18. Dr. David Albert, MD, CEO, AliveCor, phone interview with the author, January 16, 2018

19. "AliveCor Granted Patent for Proactive Notification of Possible Heart Arrhythmias," Alivecor, December 12, 2017. https://www.alivecor.com/press/press_release/alivecor-granted-patent-for-proactive-notification-of-possible-heart-arrhythmias/

20. Dr. J. Christian Fox, "Testimonials," *Butterfly IQ*. https://www.butterflynetwork.com/testimonials

21. "Meet iQ: Whole Body Imaging for Under $2K," Butterfly Network. https://www.butterflynetwork.com/

22. James Manyika, Michael Chui, Peter Bisson, et al, "The Internet of Things: Mapping the Value Beyond the Hype," McKinsey Global Institute, June, 2015. https://www.mckinsey.com/~/media/McKinsey/Business%20Functions/McKinsey%20Digital/Our%20Insights/The%20Internet%20of%20Things%20The%20value%20of%20digitizing%20the%20physical%20world/The-Internet-of-things-Mapping-the-value-beyond-the-hype.ashx

23. Andrew Liszewski, "L'Oréal's Smart Hairbrush Knows More About Your Hair Than Your Salon Does." *Gizmodo*, January 3, 2017.https://gizmodo.com/l-ore-al-s-smart-hairbrush-knows-more-about-your-hair-t-1790588112; David Rose, *Enchanted*

Objects: Design, Human Desire, and the Internet of Things,
Scribner. Kindle Edition.

24. Ibid., p. 47.
25. Ibid.
26. Conner Forrest, "Hidden U.S. Military Bases Revealed by Fitness App, Shows Need for IoT Policy," *TechRepublic*, January 29, 2018. https://www.techrepublic.com/article/hidden-us-military-bases-revealed-by-fitness-app-shows-need-for-iot-policy/
27. "IoT Design Manifesto 1.0." https://www.iotmanifesto.com/
28. Bret Kinsella, "Amazon Echo and Alexa Stats," *Voicebot.ai.* https://www.voicebot.ai/amazon-echo-alexa-stats/
29. "Amazon.Com Announces Fourth Quarter Sales Up 38% to $60.5 Billion." http://phx.corporate-ir.net/phoenix.zhtml?c=97664&p=irol-reportsother
30. W. David Stephenson, "SmartAging," *Stephenson Blogs on Internet of Things.* http://www.stephensonstrategies.com/?s=SmartAging
31. "Programs Itself, Then Pays for Itself," Nest. https://nest.com/thermostats/nest-learning-thermostat/overview/
32. Sami Grover, "Nest Aims to Provide 1 Million Smart Thermostats to Low-Income Families," *Treehugger*, January 9, 2018. https://www.treehugger.com/energy-efficiency/nest-aims-provide-1-million-smart-thermostats-low-income-families.html
33. "Learn More About Rush Hour Rewards." https://nest.com/support/article/What-is-Rush-Hour-Rewards
34. Nick Statt, "Nest Is Rejoining Google to Better Compete with Amazon and Apple," *The Verge,* February 7, 2018. https://www.theverge.com/2018/2/7/16987002/nest-google-alphabet-smart-home-competition-amazon-alexa-apple
35. Dr. David Albert, interview with author, January 16, 2018.
36. "Apple Watch Is the Highest Selling Wearable in Q3 2017 with a 23% Market Share, Says Canalys report," *Tech2*, November 15, 2017. http://www.firstpost.com/tech/news-analysis/apple-watch-is-the-highest-selling-wearable-in-q3-2017-with-a-23-market-share-says-canalys-report-4210361.html; author's note: I work part-time for Apple on the retail level. In that role I am not privy to any strategy or decision making.
37. Jennifer Newton, "Teenage Football Player's Life Is Saved by His Apple Watch After It Showed His Heart Rate Was Dan-

gerously High," *Daily Mail*, September 23, 2015. The teen not only recovered but was also offered an internship with Apple. http://www.dailymail.co.uk/news/article-3246154/Teenage-football-player-s-life-saved-Apple-Watch-showed-heart-rate-dangerously-high.html#ixzz56odiUKGr

38. Sarah Buhr. "The Apple Watch Can Detect Diabetes with an 85% Accuracy, Cardiogram Study Says," *TechCrunch*, February 7, 2018. https://techcrunch.com/2018/02/07/the-apple-watch-can-detect-diabetes-with-an-85-accuracy-cardiogram-study-says/

39. Darrell Etherington, "Philips Debuts Open APIs And An iOS SDK For Hue Connected Lighting System," *TechCrunch*, March 10, 2013. https://techcrunch.com/2013/03/10/philips-hue-lighting-sdk-ios/

40. "Philips Hue," *IFTTT*. https://ifttt.com/hue

41. Ry Crist, "New Study Details a Security Flaw with Philips Hue Smart Bulbs," *C|NET*, November 3, 2016. https://www.cnet.com/news/new-study-details-a-security-flaw-with-philips-hue-smart-bulbs/

CHAPTER 7

1. Porter and Heppelmann, *op.cit.*

2. Ginger Christ, "2013 IW Best Plants Winner: Harley-Davidson—Driving a Future of Excellence," *Industry Week*, January 12, 2014.

3. Paul Smith, "Harley Davidson to Layoff 118 From York Plant," *Fox 43*, April 12, 2017. http://fox43.com/2017/04/20/harley-to-layoff-118-employees-in-york/

4. "SAP Digital Manufacturing Rapid-deployment Solution," SAP. https://www.sap.com/services/rapid-deployment/connected-manufacturing.html

5. "The LM Vision," Local Motors. https://localmotors.com/company/http://www.industryweek.com/manufacturing-leader-week/hp-deloitte-team-transform-manufacturing

6. "The OSRAM Ticket Manager," Bosch Software Innovations. https://www.bosch-si.com/manufacturing/insights/i40-references/osram.html

7. Jade Fell, "Hannover 2017: IoT-enabled App Engine Customizes Operations on the Shop Floor," *E & T: Engineering &*

Technology, April 27, 2017. https://eandt.theiet.org/content/
articles/2017/04/hannover-2017-iot-enabled-app-engine-
customises-operations-on-the-shop-floor/

8. "Tulip Announced the Manufacturing App Platform," Press
release, April 24, 2017. https://tulip.co/press-release

9. Ibid.

10. Eric Bender, "Apps for Operators on the Factory Floor," MIT
Industrial Liaison Program, December 5, 2016. https://ilp.mit
.edu/newsstory.jsp?id=22700

11. "New Balance Digitally Reduces Defects," Tulip news release.
https://tulip.co/case-studies/nb

12. Bender, *op.cit.*

13. The Forrester Wave: "Low-Code Development Platforms For
AD&D Pros, Q4 2017." https://www.mendix.com/resources/
forrester-low-code-development-platforms-q4-2017-mx/?utm_
source=google&utm_medium=cpc&utm_term=no%20code&
utm_campaign=NA%20-%20Low%20Code&gclid=CjwKCAi
A78XTBRBiEiwAGv7EKpI5O1rJ44Rr6pDs6A0DgTEepJlVW
ejJFdkpe0GUwQn8R3dY0bYDOBoCMNoQAvD_BwE; Author's note: I ran a webinar for Mendix.

14. Ibid.

15. Michael Hobbs, "The Connected Industrial Worker: Achieving
the Industrial Vision for the Internet of Things," Advertising
content, Accenture Digital, January 23, 2017. http://www
.telegraph.co.uk/business/digital-leaders/horizons/telegraph-
horizons-connected-industrial-worker/

16. John Santagate, "The Human Touch in Smart Manufacturing,"
IDC Community, February 14, 2017. https://idc-community.
com/manufacturing/manufacturing-value-chain/the_human_
touch_in_smart_manufacturing?utm_content=buffer09ca8
&utm_medium=social&utm_source=twitter.com&utm_
campaign=buffer

17. Stephenson, *Data Dynamite, op.cit.*

18. Asín, *op.cit.*

19. Porter and Heppelmann, *op.cit.*

20. UX Collective. https://uxdesign.cc/the-product-design-of-iot-
b4f13305c852

21. Suketu Gandhi and Eric Gervet, "Now That Your Products
Can Talk, What Will They Tell You?" *MIT Sloan Management*

Review, Spring 2016. https://sloanreview.mit.edu/article/now-that-your-products-can-talk-what-will-they-tell-you/

22. Hardy, *op.cit.*
23. Gandhi and Gervet, "Now That Your Products Can Talk, What Will They Tell You?"
24. Porter and Heppelmann, *op.cit.*
25. Gandhi and Gervet, "Now That Your Products Can Talk, What Will They Tell You?"
26. Kaan Turnali, "What Is Design Thinking?" *Forbes/SAP Voice*, May 18, 2015. https://www.forbes.com/sites/sap/2015/05/10/what-is-design-thinking/
27. Jeremy Rifkin, *The Zero Marginal Cost Society: The Internet of Things, the Collaborative Commons, and the Eclipse of Capitalism*, New York: St. Martin's Press, 2014. p. 219.
28. Office of the Press Secretary, "Fact Sheet: Obama Administration Announces Columbus, OH Winner of the $40 Million Smart City Challenge to Pioneer the Future of Transportation." White House, June 23, 2016. https://obamawhitehouse.archives.gov/the-press-office/2016/06/23/fact-sheet-obama-administration-announces-columbus-oh-winner-40-million
29. Ohio Department of Transportation, "Smart Mobility Corridor to Become Ohio's First 'Smart Road,'" State of Ohio. https://www.dot.state.oh.us/news/PagesSmartMobilityCorridor.aspx
30. Contributor, "Why Retail Giant Coca-Cola Is Using IoT Connected Vending Machines," *Internet of Business*, September 16, 2016. https://internetofbusiness.com/supply-chain-iot-coca-cola/
31. Jon-Amerin Vorabutra, "Why Blockchain is a Game Changer for Supply Chain Management," *LoadDelivered*, Jan. 28, 2016. https://www.loaddelivered.com/blog/why-blockchain-is-a-game-changer-for-supply-chain-management/
32. Ibid.
33. Helen Saunders, "Blockchain: A New Paradigm for Supply Chain Security?," *Cisco UK and Ireland Blog*, April 28, 2017. https://gblogs.cisco.com/uki/blockchain-a-new-paradigm-for-supply-chain-security/
34. Eric Free, "Tesla: Driving the new Industrial Revolution," *IoT Agenda*, December 19, 2016. http://internetofthingsagenda

.techtarget.com/blog/IoT-Agenda/Tesla-Driving-the-new-Industrial-Revolution

35. Ibid.

36. Robert Thomson, Madelaine Edwards, Emma Britton, Bryan Rabenau, "Is the Timing Right for Predictive Maintenance in the Manufacturing Sector?," *Think Act Magazine,* November 2014. http://studylib.net/doc/18212956/predictive-maintenance#

37. Stefano Marinotti, Jim Nolten, and Arne Steinsbø, "Digitizing Oil and Gas Production," McKinsey & Co. Oil and Gas, August, 2014. "https://www.mckinsey.com/industries/oil-and-gas/our-insights/digitizing-oil-and-gas-production

38. Thomson, *et.al, op.cit.* The benefits could stretch even further. After the horrific Deep Water Horizon explosion in 2010, I wrote an op-ed in *Federal Computer Week* arguing that 24/7 monitoring of wells could also lead to what I called "Regulation 2.0," in which, with appropriate safeguards for company secrets, etc., the government could share the realtime data and be able to respond more rapidly in a disaster. Even without a step, realtime data will simplify reporting, and will dramatically reduce the chance of blowouts with their accompanying costs for all concerned. W. David Stephenson, "Future Oil Spills Could Be Averted by Regulation 3.0 apps," *Federal Computer Week*, June 2, 2010. https://fcw.com/Articles/2010/06/07/COMMENT-David-Stephenson-Regulation-transparency.aspx

39. "Fueling the Oil and Gas Industry with IoT," *Microsoft Customer Stories*, July 26, 2015. https://customers.microsoft.com/en-us/story/fueling-the-oil-and-gas-industry-with-iot-1

40. Stefano Martinotti, Jim Nolten, and Jens Arne Steinsbo, "Digitizing oil and gas production," *McKinsey*, August, 2014. https://www.mckinsey.com/industries/oil-and-gas/our-insights/digitizing-oil-and-gas-production

41. Ibid.

42. Ibid.

43. Woodrow Bellamy III, "OEMs Embrace New Aircraft Engine Health Monitoring Tech," *Avionics*, February 15, 2017. http://www.aviationtoday.com/2017/02/15/oems-embrace-new-aircraft-engine-health-monitoring-tech/

44. "Pratt & Whitney Applies 'Big Data' to Predict Engine Maintenance Frequency and Planning," Pratt & Whitney (News release), February 16, 2016. https://www.prnewswire.com/news-releases/pratt--whitney-applies-big-data-to-predict-engine-maintenance-frequency-and-planning-300220490.html

45. Bhoopathi Rapolu, "Internet Of Aircraft Things: An Industry Set To Be Transformed," *Aviation Week*, January 18, 2016. http://aviationweek.com/connected-aerospace/internet-aircraft-things-industry-set-be-transformed

46. Guest Contributor, "How IoT Technologies Are Disrupting the Aerospace and Defence Status Quo," *IT ProPortal*, October 27, 2016. https://www.itproportal.com/features/how-iot-technologies-are-disrupting-the-aerospace-and-defence-status-quo/

CHAPTER 8

1. Porter and Heppelman, *op.cit.*

2. Charles F. O'Connor, Jr., *Military Enterprise and Technological Change: Perspectives on the American Experience,* MIT Press, 1985, p. 90. https://books.google.com/books?id=ukk6jtvWtMoC&pg=PA90&lpg=PA90&dq=early+railroad+disaster+and+army&source=bl&ots=HOJ6KLEcAg&sig=Rjxto27TBkJBvAKUQJm9Tg727_E&hl=en&sa=X&ved=0ahUKEwjT3e3tzNzYAhWvS98KHWakDwE4ChDoAQguMAE#v=onepage&q=early%20railroad%20disaster%20and%20army&f=false

3. Thomas S. Kuhn, *The Structure of Scientific,* 2nd edition. International Encyclopedia of Unified Science. Chicago: University of Chicago, 1970.

4. Ibid., pp. 89–90.

5. Gary Hamel, "Innovation Democracy: W. L. Gore's Original Management Model," *Management Innovation eXchange*, September 23, 2010. http://www.managementexchange.com/story/innovation-democracy-wl-gores-original-management-model

6. Alan Deutchman, "The Fabric of Creativity," *Fast Company*, December 1, 2004. https://www.fastcompany.com/51733/fabric-creativity

7. Cathy Benko and Molly Anderson, "The Lattice That Has

Replaced The Corporate Ladder," *Forbes*, March 16, 2011. https://www.forbes.com/2011/03/16/corporate-lattice-ladder-leadership-managing-hierarchy.html#25874a183228

8. Russell J. Ackoff, "The Circular Organization: An Update," *The Academy of Management Executive*, February 1989. https://www.jstor.org/stable/4164862

9. Ann Augustine, "A Review of the Slack Communication Service," *LifeWire*, July 5, 2017. https://www.lifewire.com/slack-sets-standard-team-communication-online-771603

10. "5 Benefits of Collaboration in the Workplace," *IngramMicro Advisor*. http://www.ingrammicroadvisor.com/unified-communications-and-collaboration/5-benefits-of-collaboration-in-the-workplace

11. Jayraj Nair, "3 Ways Business Can Use IoT to Save the Environment," *WinPro*. http://wiprodigital.com/2018/01/18/3-ways-businesses-can-use-iot-to-save-the-environment/

12. "How Collaboration Wins," *Harvard Business Review* Analytical Services, January 2018. https://hbr.org/resources/pdfs/comm/citrix/HowCollaborationWins.pdf

13. Ibid.

INDEX

Index